WORD 6
FOR WINDOWS™

V I S U A L

PocketGuide

by: maranGraphics' Development Group

IDG BOOKS

IDG Books Worldwide, Inc.
An International Data Group Company

San Mateo, California ✦ Indianapolis, Indiana ✦ Boston, Massachusetts

Word 6 for Windows™ Visual PocketGuide

Published by
IDG Books Worldwide, Inc.
An International Data Group Company
155 Bovet Road, Suite 310
San Mateo, CA 94402
(415) 312-0650

Copyright© 1994 by maranGraphics Inc.,
5755 Coopers Avenue
Mississauga, Ontario, Canada
L4Z 1R9

Screen shot(s) reprinted
with permission from
Microsoft Corporation.

Library of Congress Catalog Card No.: 94-079406

ISBN: 1-56884-666-5

Printed in the United States of America

10 9 8 7 6 5 4 3

Distributed in the United States by IDG Books Worldwide, Inc.

Distributed by Computer and Technical Books in Miami, Florida, fo‑
South America and the Caribbean; by Longman Singapore in Singapore
Malaysia, Thailand, and Korea; by Toppan Co. Ltd. in Japan; by Asi‑
Computerworld in Hong Kong; by Woodslane Pty. Ltd. in Australia an‑
New Zealand; and by Transworld Publishers Ltd. in the U.K. and Ireland.

For general information on IDG Books in the U.S., including informatio‑
on discounts and premiums, contact IDG Books at 800-762-297‑
or 317-895-5200.

For U.S. Corporate Sales and quantity discounts, contact maranGraphic‑
at 800-469-6616, ext. 206.

For information on international sales of IDG Books, contact Christina Turne‑
at 415-312-0633.

For information on translations, contact Marc Jeffrey Mikulich, Foreig‑
Rights Manager, at IDG Books Worldwide. Fax Number 415-286-2747.

For sales inquiries and special prices for bulk quantities, write to th‑
address above or call IDG Books Worldwide at 415-312-0650.

For information on using IDG Books in the classroom, or orderin‑
examination copies, contact Jim Kelly at 800-434-2086.

Trademark Acknowledgments

maranGraphics Inc. has attempted to include trademark information for products, services and companies referred to in this guide. Although maranGraphics Inc. has made reasonable efforts in gathering this information, it cannot guarantee its accuracy.

Microsoft, MS, MS-DOS and Microsoft Mouse are registered trademarks, and Windows is a trademark of Microsoft Corporation.

©1994
maranGraphics, Inc.

The animated characters are the
copyright of maranGraphics, Inc.

iv

About IDG Books Worldwide

Welcome to the world of IDG Books Worldwide.

IDG Books Worldwide, Inc., is a subsidiary of International Data Group, the worl
largest publisher of business and computer-related information and the leading g
provider of information services on information technology. IDG was founded mo
than 25 years ago and now employs more than 5,700 people worldwide. IDG
publishes more than 200 computer publications in 63 countries (see listing below
Forty million people read one or more IDG publications each month.

Launched in 1990, IDG Books is today the fastest-growing publisher of computer
and business books in the United States. We are proud to have received 3 awards
from the Computer Press Association in recognition of editorial excellence, and o
best-selling ...For Dummies series has more than 10 million copies in print with
translations in more than 20 languages. IDG Books, through a recent joint ventur
with IDG's Hi-Tech Beijing, became the first U.S. publisher to publish a compute
book in the People's Republic of China. In record time, IDG Books has become th
first choice for millions of readers around the world who want to learn how to be
manage their businesses.

Our mission is simple: Every IDG book is designed to bring extra value and skill-
building instructions to the reader. Our books are written by experts who unders
and care about our readers. The knowledge base of our editorial staff comes from
years of experience in publishing, education, and journalism — experience which
use to produce books for the '90s. In short, we care about books, so we attract th
best people. We devote special attention to details such as audience, interior desi
use of icons, and illustrations. And because we use an efficient process of authori
editing, and desktop publishing our books electronically, we can spend more tim
ensuring superior content and spend less time on the technicalities of making bo

You can count on our commitment to deliver high-quality books at competitive
prices on topics customers want to read about. At IDG, we value quality, and we
have been delivering quality for more than 25 years. You'll find no better book o
subject than an IDG book.

John Kilcullen
President and CEO
IDG Books Worldwide, Inc.

IDG Books Worldwide, Inc., is a subsidiary of International Data Group. The officers are Patrick J. McGovern, Founder and Board Chairman; Walter Boyd
International Data Group's publications include: ARGENTINA'S Computerworld Argentina, Infoworld Argentina; AUSTRALIA'S Computerworld Australia, Au
World, Australian Macworld, Network World, Mobile Business Australia, Reseller, IDG Sources; AUSTRIA'S Computerwelt Oesterreich, PC Test;
Computerworld, Gamepro, Game Power, Mundo IBM, Mundo Unix, PC World, Super Game; BELGIUM'S Data News (CW) BULGARIA'S Computerworl
Ediworld, PC & Mac World Bulgaria, Network World Bulgaria; CANADA'S CIO Canada, Computerworld Canada, Graduate Computerworld, InfoCanada, Netw
Canada; CHILE'S Computerworld Chile, Informatica; COLOMBIA'S Computerworld Colombia, PC World; CZECH REPUBLIC'S Computerworld, Elektronika
DENMARK'S Communications World, Computerworld Danmark, Macintosh Produktkatalog, Macworld Danmark, PC World Danmark, PC World Produktg
World, Windows World; ECUADOR'S PC World Ecuador; EGYPT'S Computerworld (CW) Middle East, PC World Middle East; FINLAND'S MikroPC,
Tietoverkko; FRANCE'S Distributique, GOLDEN MAC, InfoPC, Languages & Systems, Le Guide du Monde Informatique, Le Monde Informatique, Telecoms
GERMANY'S Computerwoche, Computerwoche Focus, Computerwoche Extra, Computerwoche Karriere, Information Management, Macwelt, Netzwelt, PC
Woche, Publish, Unit; GREECE'S Infoworld, PC Games; HUNGARY'S Computerworld SZT, PC World; HONG KONG'S Computerworld Hong Kong, PC W
Kong; INDIA'S Computers & Communications; IRELAND'S ComputerScope; ISRAEL'S Computerworld Israel, PC World Israel; ITALY'S Computerworld
Magazine, Macworld Italia, Networking Italia, PC Shopping, PC World Italia; JAPAN'S Computerworld Today, Information Systems World, Macworld Ja
Personal Computing, SunWorld Japan, Windows World; KENYA'S East African Computer News; KOREA'S Computerworld Korea, Macworld Korea, PC W
MEXICO'S Compu Edicion, Compu Manufactura, Computacion/Punto de Venta, Computerworld Mexico, MacWorld, Mundo Unix, PC World, Win
NETHERLANDS' Computer! Totaal, Computable (CW), LAN Magazine, MacWorld, Totaal "Windows"; NEW ZEALAND'S Computer Listings, Computer
Zealand, New Zealand PC World, Network World; NIGERIA'S PC World Africa; NORWAY'S Computerworld Norge, C/World, Lotusworld Norge, Macwo
Networld, PC World Ekspress, PC World Norge, PC World's Produktguide, Publish& Multimedia World, Student Data, Unix World, Windowsworld;
Response; PAKISTAN'S PC World Pakistan; PANAMA'S PC World Panama; PERU'S Computerworld Peru, PC World; PEOPLE'S REPUBLIC OF CHI
Computerworld, China Infoworld, Electronics Today/Multimedia World, Electronics International, Electronic Product World, China Network Wor
Communications Magazine, PC World China, Software World Magazine, Telecom Product World; IDG HIGH TECH BEIJING'S New Product World; IDG SH
Computer News Digest; PHILIPPINES' Computerworld Philippines, PC Digest (PCW); POLAND'S Computerworld Poland, PC World/Komputer; PC
Cerebro/PC World, Correio Informatico/Computerworld, Informatica & Comunicacoes Catalogo, MacIn, Nacional de Produtos; ROMANIA'S Computerworld
RUSSIA'S Computerworld-Moscow, Mir - PC, Sety; SINGAPORE'S Computerworld Southeast Asia, PC World Singapore; SLOVENIA'S Monitor Magazi
AFRICA'S Computer Mail (CIO),Computing S.A.,Network World S.A., Software World; SPAIN'S Advanced Systems, Amiga World, Computerwor
Communicaciones World, Macworld Espana, NeXTWORLD, Super Juegos Magazine (GamePro), PC World Espana, Publish; SWEDEN'S Attack, Comp
Corporate Computing, Natverk & Kommunikation, Macworld, Mikrodatorn, PC World, Publishing & Design (CAP), Datalngenjoren, Maxi Data,Wind
SWITZERLAND'S Computerworld Schweiz, Macworld Schweiz, PC Tip; TAIWAN'S Computerworld Taiwan, PC World Taiwan; THAILAND'S Thai Com
TURKEY'S Computerworld Monitor, Macworld Turkiye, PC World Turkiye; UKRAINE'S Computerworld; UNITED KINGDOM'S Computing /Com
Connexion/Network World, Lotus Magazine, Macworld, Open Computing/Sunworld; UNITED STATES' Advanced Systems, AmigaWorld, Cable in the Cla
Review, CIO, Computerworld, Digital Video, DOS Resource Guide, Electronic Entertainment Magazine, Federal Computer Week, Federal Integrator, Ga
Books, Infoworld, Infoworld Direct, Laser Event, Macworld, Multimedia World, Network World, PC Letter, PC World, PlayRight, Power PC World, Publish
Video Event; VENEZUELA'S Computerworld Venezuela, PC World; VIETNAM'S PC World Vietnam

Acknowledgments

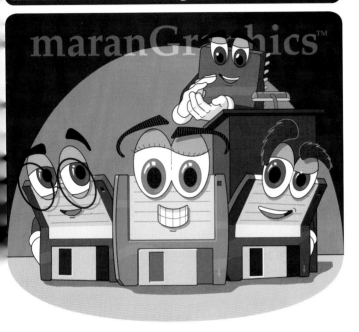

Thanks to Hilaire Gagne and Matthew Price of Microsoft Canada Inc. for their support and consultation.

Special thanks to Wendi B. Ewbank for her patience, insight and humor throughout the project.

Thanks to José F. Pérez and Saverio C. Tropiano for their assistance and expert advice.

Thanks to the dedicated staff of maranGraphics including, Peters Ezers, David de Haas, David Hendricks, Jill Maran, Judy Maran, Maxine Maran, Robert Maran, Dave Ross, Christie Van Duin, Carol Walthers and Kelleigh Wing.

Finally, to Richard Maran who originated the easy-to-use graphic format of this guide. Thank you for your inspiration and guidance.

Credits

Author:
Ruth Maran

Consultant:
Wendi Blouin Ewbank

Layout Artist:
Carol Walthers

Designer:
David de Haas

Illustrator:
Dave Ross

Production Editor:
Kelleigh Wing

Editor:
Judy Maran

Post Production:
Robert Maran

TABLE OF CONTENTS

TABLE OF CONTENTS

INTRODUCTION

A typewriter makes editing your document a difficult task. If you want to make minor changes, you have to use correction fluid. For extensive changes, you may even have to retype your entire document.

Microsoft® Word 6.0 for Windows™ enables you to produce documents in less time and with greater accuracy. You can take advantage of the editing and formatting features provided to produce impressive-looking documents.

This is what you can create with Word for Windows.

Thesis on Narcolepsy: Lying Down Rather A Lot

Jim Leung
M.B.A., D.O.A.
University of Washington

REPORTS AND MANUALS

Word for Windows provides editing and formatting features that make it ideal for producing longer documents such as reports and manuals.

MAILING LISTS

Word for Windows can merge documents with a list of names and addresses to produce personalized letters.

Mailing List 1994

Mr. Wayne Abacus 345 Luton Street Fullerton, California 92740	Mr. Mycroft Merril 349 Hardwich Drive Toronto, Ontario L5C 3E3
Mr. Yvon Crispin 2121 Pourquoi Lane Montreal, Quebec L5N 3E3	Mrs. Edith Preston 57 Enmount Drive Delkierton, Maine 45678
Mr. Arthur Dent 78 Drury Lane Paxton, Illinois 23456	Mr. George Sarent 26 June Street Golgofrincham, Alabama 34567
Mrs. Mary Ducas 450 Ukelele Court Seattle, Washington 78899	Mrs. Nathalie Schwartz 3 Knightsbridge Lane Simmons, California 90210
Mr. Conrad Fennelly 8 Evergreen Avenue Chicago, Illinois 12345	Ms. Jan Torbram 205 Vodden Street Trillium, Wisconsin 45678
Mrs. Barb Hewitson 100 Grange Drive Buffalo, New York 34567	Mr. Marvin Williams 1 Para Crescent Nold, Georgia 23560
Mr. Keith Lovejoy 7 Lorraine Cresecent Boston, Massachusetts 67890	Mrs. Kathleen Wong 1267 Woodbridge Street Pasterville, Maine 34589

PERSONAL AND BUSINESS LETTERS

Word for Windows helps you to produce letters quickly and accurately.

January 12, 1994

ABC Computer Corporation
P.O. Box 2501
Krikkit, VA 22106

Re: Position Opening-Receptionist

To whom it may concern:

Regarding your advertisement of January 9, 1994, I am pleased to submit my résumé for review and wish to be considered as an applicant for the above-named position.

My professional experience does include using Word. I am well versed in the program capabilities and able to apply the features accurately. Should you find my background and qualifications acceptable, I would be delighted to interview for this position at your convenience.

Thank you for your assistance in this matter. I look forward to discussing this career opportunity with you.

Sincerely yours,

Susan Johnston

Susan Johnston
enclosure

MOUSE BASICS

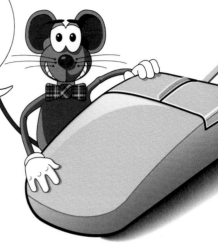

The mouse is a hand-held device that lets you quickly select commands and perform tasks.

USING THE MOUSE

Hold the mouse as shown in the diagram. Use your thumb and two rightmost fingers to guide the mouse while your two remaining fingers press the mouse buttons.

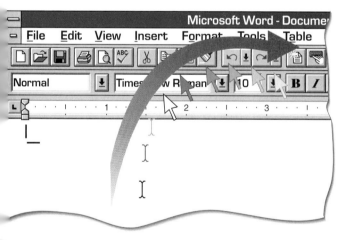

When you move the mouse on your desk, the mouse pointer ($\&$ or I) on your screen also moves. The mouse pointer changes shape depending on its location on your screen.

MOUSE BASICS

◆ The mouse has a left and right button. You can use these buttons to:

- open menus
- select commands
- choose options

Note: You will use the left button most of the time.

MOUSE TERMS

CLICK

Quickly press and release the left mouse button once.

DOUBLE-CLICK

Quickly press and release the left mouse button twice.

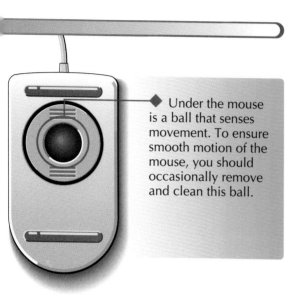

◆ Under the mouse is a ball that senses movement. To ensure smooth motion of the mouse, you should occasionally remove and clean this ball.

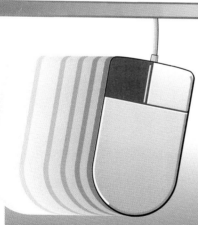

DRAG

When the mouse pointer (⬉ or I) is over an object on your screen, press and hold down the left mouse button and then move the mouse.

START WORD

When you start Word for Windows, a blank document appears.

 START WORD FOR WINDOWS

C:\> WIN_

1 To start Word for Windows from MS-DOS, type **WIN** and then press **Enter**.

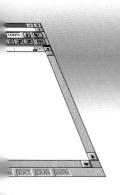

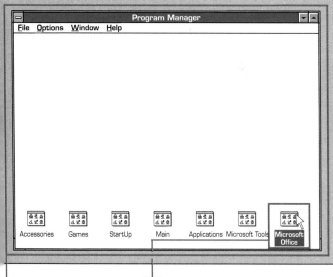

◆ The **Program
Manager** window
appears.

2 To open the group window
that contains Word, move the
mouse ↳ over the icon (example:
Microsoft Office) and then quickly
press the left button twice.

Note: To continue, refer to the next page.

11

START WORD

You can type text into the document displayed on your screen.

START WORD (Continued)

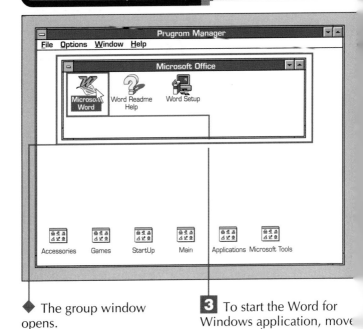

◆ The group window opens.

3 To start the Word for Windows application, move the mouse ⌖ over **Microsoft Word** and then quickly press the left button twice.

12

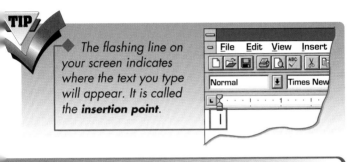

TIP

◆ The flashing line on your screen indicates where the text you type will appear. It is called the **insertion point**.

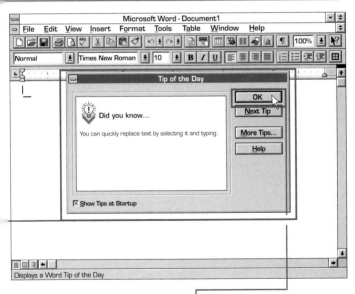

◆ The **Microsoft Word** window appears, displaying a blank document.

◆ Each time you start Word, a tip about using the program appears.

4 To close the **Tip of the Day** dialog box, move the mouse ⌖ over **OK** and then press the left button.

13

ENTER TEXT

When typing text in your document you do not need to press Enter at the end of a line. Word automatically moves the text to the next line. This is called word wrapping.

ENTER TEXT

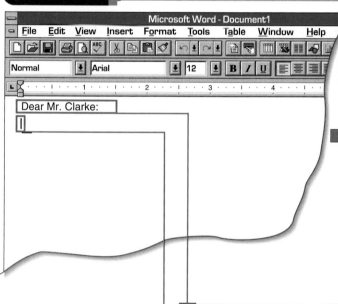

Microsoft Word - Document1

File   Edit   View   Insert   Format   Tools   Table   Window   Help

Normal   Arial   12   B I U

Dear Mr. Clarke:

◆ The flashing line (|) on your screen indicates where the text you type will appear. It is called the **insertion point**.

1 Type the first line of text.

2 To start a new line, press Enter.

3 To start a new paragraph press Enter again.

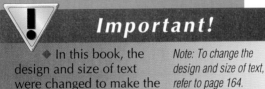

Important!

◆ In this book, the design and size of text were changed to make the document easier to read.

Note: To change the design and size of text, refer to page 164.

Initial or default font	➤	New font
Times New Roman 10 point		Arial 12 point

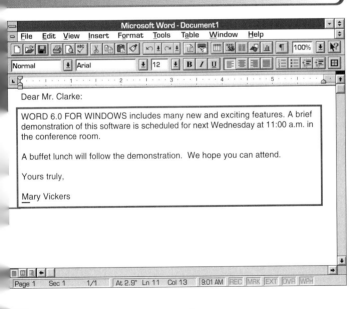

Dear Mr. Clarke:

WORD 6.0 FOR WINDOWS includes many new and exciting features. A brief demonstration of this software is scheduled for next Wednesday at 11:00 a.m. in the conference room.

A buffet lunch will follow the demonstration. We hope you can attend.

Yours truly,

Mary Vickers

4 Type the remaining text.

◆ Press **Enter** only when you want to start a new line or paragraph.

15

THE STATUS BAR

THE STATUS BAR

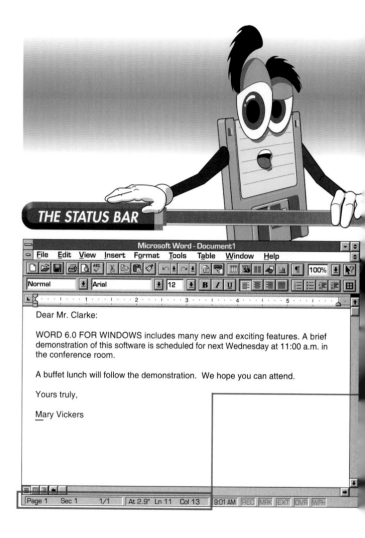

The Status bar provides information about the position of the insertion point and the text displayed on your screen.

◆ **Page 1**
The page displayed on your screen.

◆ **Sec 1**
The section of the document displayed on your screen.

◆ **1/1**
The page displayed on your screen/The total number of pages in your document.

◆ **At 2.9"**
The distance (in inches) from the top of the page to the insertion point.

◆ **Ln 11**
The number of lines from the top of the page to the insertion point.

◆ **Col 13**
The number of characters from the left margin to the insertion point, including spaces.

SELECT COMMANDS

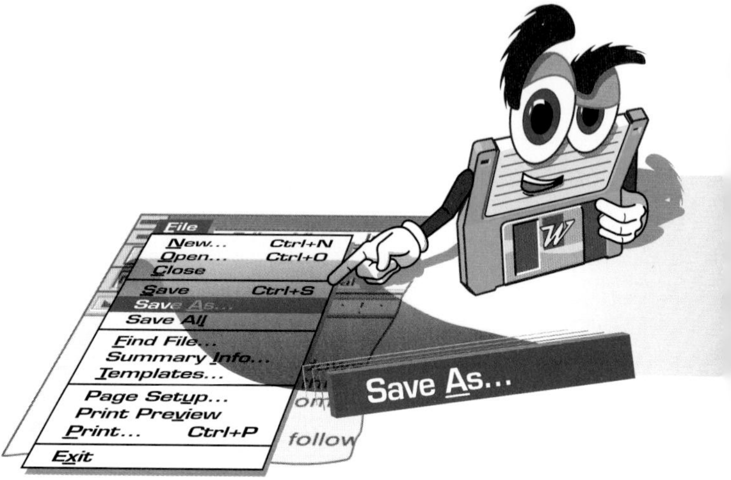

USING THE MOUSE

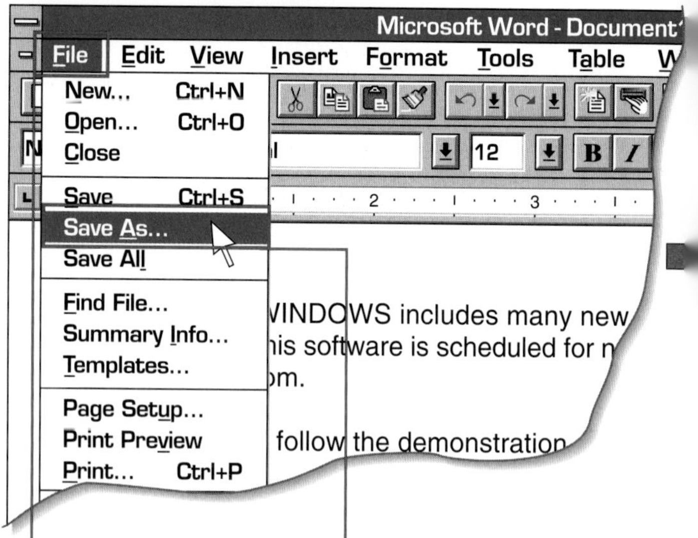

1 To open a menu, move the mouse over the menu name (example: **File**) and then press the left button.

◆ A menu appears displaying a list of related commands.

Note: To close a menu, move the mouse anywhere over your document and then press the left button.

2 To select a command, move the mouse over the command name (example: **Save As**) and then press the left button.

You can open
a menu to display a
list of related commands.
You can then select
the command you
want to use.

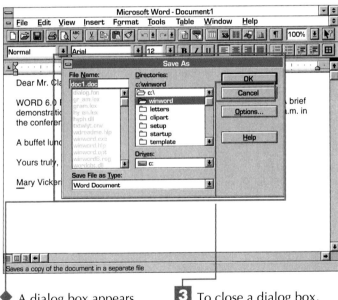

◆ A dialog box appears
if Word requires more
information to carry out
the command.

3 To close a dialog box,
move the mouse ⤄ over
Cancel and then press the
left button.

SELECT COMMANDS

You can use the keyboard to select a command.

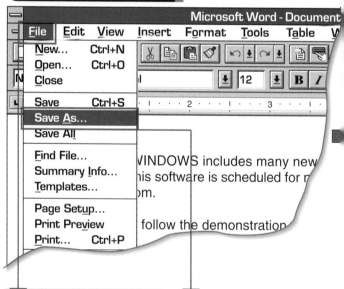

Microsoft Word - Document

File | Edit | View | Insert | Format | Tools | Table | W

New... Ctrl+N
Open... Ctrl+O
Close

Save Ctrl+S
Save As...
Save All

Find File...
Summary Info...
Templates...

Page Setup...
Print Preview
Print... Ctrl+P

12 | B | I

· · · 2 · · · | · · · 3 · · · | · ·

WINDOWS includes many new
his software is scheduled for r
om.

follow the demonstration

1 To open a menu, press `Alt` followed by the underlined letter in the menu name (example: `F` for **File**).

Note: To close a menu, press `Alt`.

2 To select a command, press the underlined letter in the command name (example `A` for **Save As**).

20

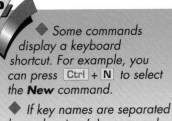

◆ Some commands display a keyboard shortcut. For example, you can press Ctrl + N to select the *New* command.

◆ If key names are separated by a plus sign (+), press and hold down the first key before pressing the second key (example: Ctrl + N).

File	
New...	Ctrl+N
Open...	Ctrl+O
Close	
Save	Ctrl+S
Save As...	
Save All	

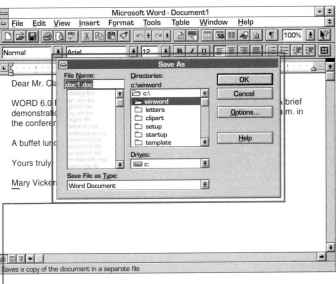

◆ A dialog box appears if Word requires more information to carry out the command.

3 To close a dialog box, press Esc .

SELECT COMMANDS

You can use the Word buttons to quickly select the most commonly used commands.

THE WORD BUTTONS

Each button displayed on your screen provides a fast method of selecting a menu command.

For example, you can use 🖫 to quickly select the **Save** command.

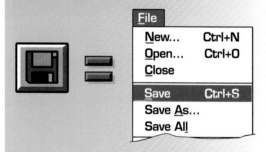

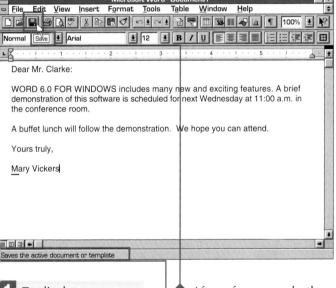

1 To display a description of a button on your screen, move the mouse over the button of interest (example: 🖫).

◆ After a few seconds, the name of the button appears (example: **Save**).

◆ A short description of the button also appears at the bottom of your screen.

MOVE THROUGH A DOCUMENT

 Important!

You cannot move the insertion point past the horizontal line (▬) displayed on your screen. To move this line, position the insertion point after the last character in your document and then press **Enter**.

If you create a long document, your computer screen cannot display all the text at the same time. You must scroll up or down to view other parts of your document.

MOVE TO ANY POSITION ON YOUR SCREEN

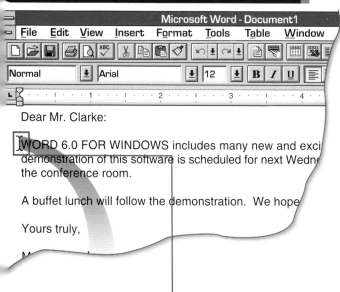

Microsoft Word - Document1

File   Edit   View   Insert   Format   Tools   Table   Window

Normal   Arial   12   **B** *I* U

Dear Mr. Clarke:

WORD 6.0 FOR WINDOWS includes many new and exci demonstration of this software is scheduled for next Wedn the conference room.

A buffet lunch will follow the demonstration. We hope

Yours truly,

The insertion point indicates where the text you type will appear in your document.

1 To position the insertion point at another location on your screen, move the mouse I over the new location and then press the left button.

25

MOVE THROUGH A DOCUMENT

SCROLL UP OR DOWN

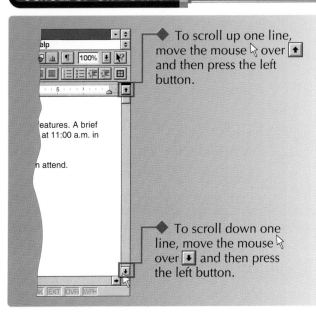

◆ To scroll up one line, move the mouse ⌖ over ⬆ and then press the left button.

◆ To scroll down one line, move the mouse ⌖ over ⬇ and then press the left button.

KEYBOARD SHORTCUTS

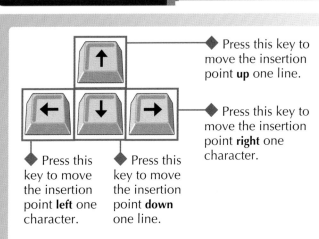

◆ Press this key to move the insertion point **up** one line.

◆ Press this key to move the insertion point **right** one character.

◆ Press this key to move the insertion point **left** one character.

◆ Press this key to move the insertion point **down** one line.

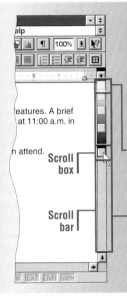

The location of the scroll box on the scroll bar indicates which part of your document is displayed on the screen.

For example, when the scroll box is in the middle of the scroll bar, you are viewing the middle part of your document.

1 To move the scroll box, position the mouse ↘ over the box and then press and hold down the left button.

2 Still holding down the button, drag the scroll box down the scroll bar. Then release the button.

 Press this key to move **up** one screen.

 Press this key to move **down** one screen.

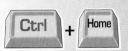 Press these keys to move to the **beginning** of your document.

 Press these keys to move to the **end** of your document.

SELECT TEXT

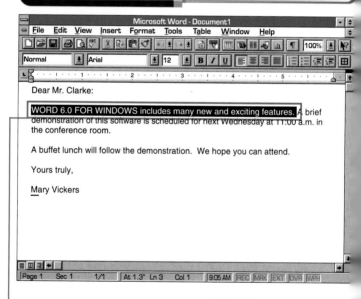

1 Press and hold down Ctrl.

2 Still holding down Ctrl, move the mouse I anywhere over the sentence you want to select and then press the left button. Release Ctrl.

TO CANCEL A TEXT SELECTION

Move the mouse I outside the selected area and then press the left button.

Before you can use many Word features, you must first select the text you want to change.

SELECT A PARAGRAPH

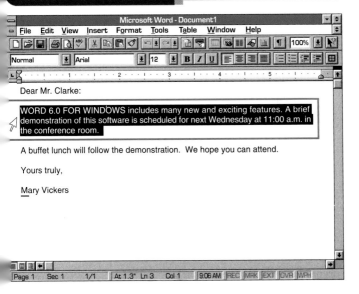

1 Move the mouse I to the left of the paragraph you want to select (I changes to ◿) and then quickly press the left button twice.

SELECT TEXT

Selected text appears highlighted on your screen.

SELECT YOUR ENTIRE DOCUMENT

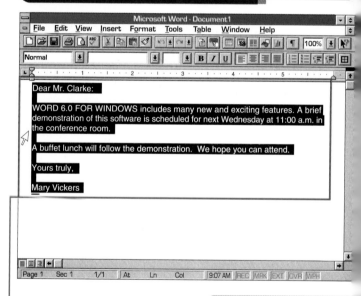

1 Move the mouse I anywhere to the left of the text in your document (I changes to ⌐⌐) and then quickly press the left button three times.

TO CANCEL A TEXT SELECTION

Move the mouse I outside the selected area and then press the left button.

SELECT A WORD

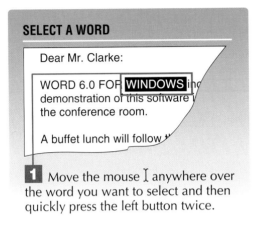

Dear Mr. Clarke:

WORD 6.0 FOR **WINDOWS** in
demonstration of this software
the conference room.

A buffet lunch will follow

1 Move the mouse I anywhere over the word you want to select and then quickly press the left button twice.

SELECT ANY AMOUNT OF TEXT

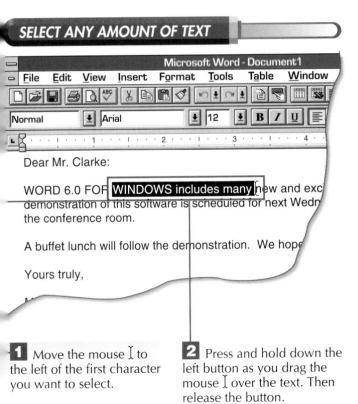

1 Move the mouse I to the left of the first character you want to select.

2 Press and hold down the left button as you drag the mouse I over the text. Then release the button.

HELP

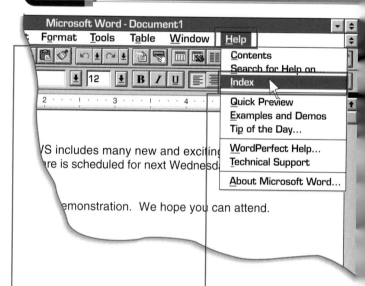

1 To display the Word Help Index, move the mouse ⌖ over **Help** and then press the left button.

2 Move the mouse ⌖ over **Index** and then press the left button.

If you forget how to perform a task, you can use the Word Help feature to obtain information.

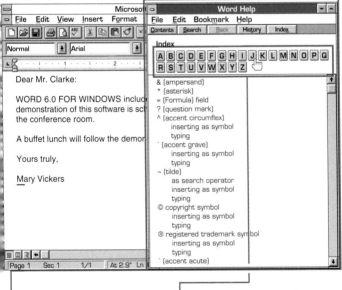

◆ The **Word Help** window appears.

3 Move the mouse 🖑 over the first letter of the topic you want information on (example: **J** for **Justification**) and then press the left button.

Note: To continue, refer to the next page.

HELP

> The Help feature can save you time by eliminating the need to refer to other sources.

HELP (Continued)

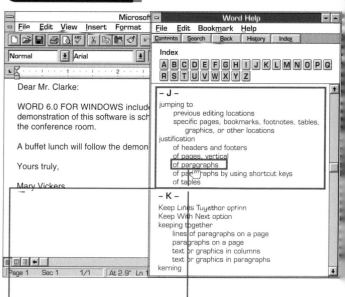

◆ Topics beginning with the letter you selected appear.

◆ To view more topics beginning with that letter, press **PageDown** on your keyboard.

4 Move the mouse 👆 over the topic of interest (example: **justification of paragraphs**) and then press the left button.

34

TIP

To print the help topic displayed on your screen:

◆ Move the mouse over ⬚ Print ⬚ in the **How To** window and then press the left button.

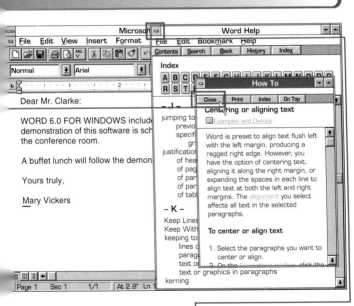

◆ Information on the topic you selected appears.

5 To close the **How To** window, move the mouse over **Close** and then press the left button.

6 To close the **Word Help** window, move the mouse over its **Control-menu** box and then quickly press the left button twice.

INSERT A BLANK LINE

INSERT A BLANK LINE

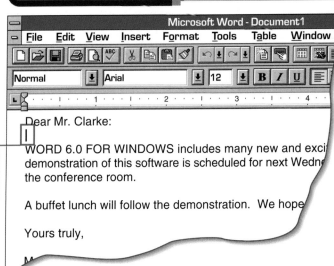

Dear Mr. Clarke:

WORD 6.0 FOR WINDOWS includes many new and exci
demonstration of this software is scheduled for next Wedn
the conference room.

A buffet lunch will follow the demonstration. We hope

Yours truly,

M

1 Position the insertion point where you want to insert a blank line.

Word makes it easy to edit your document. To make changes, you no longer have to use correction fluid or retype a page.

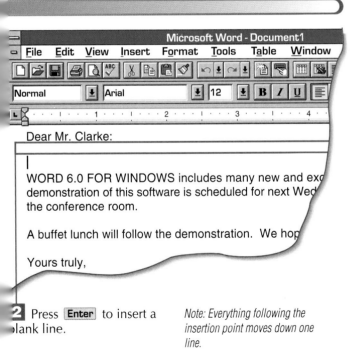

Microsoft Word - Document1

File   Edit   View   Insert   Format   Tools   Table   Window

Normal   Arial   12   B I U

Dear Mr. Clarke:

WORD 6.0 FOR WINDOWS includes many new and exc
demonstration of this software is scheduled for next Wed
the conference room.

A buffet lunch will follow the demonstration. We hop

Yours truly,

2 Press **Enter** to insert a blank line.

Note: Everything following the insertion point moves down one line.

SPLIT AND JOIN PARAGRAPHS

You can easily split or join paragraphs in your document.

SPLIT AND JOIN PARAGRAPHS

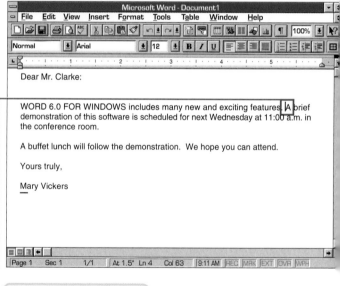

Split a Paragraph

1 Position the insertion point where you want to split a paragraph in two.

38

Important!

Make sure you save your document to store it for future use. If you do not save your document, it will disappear when you turn off your computer.

Note: To save a document, refer to page 96.

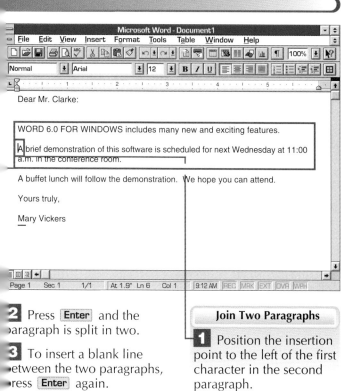

Dear Mr. Clarke:

WORD 6.0 FOR WINDOWS includes many new and exciting features.

A brief demonstration of this software is scheduled for next Wednesday at 11:00 a.m. in the conference room.

A buffet lunch will follow the demonstration. We hope you can attend.

Yours truly,

Mary Vickers

2 Press **Enter** and the paragraph is split in two.

3 To insert a blank line between the two paragraphs, press **Enter** again.

Join Two Paragraphs

1 Position the insertion point to the left of the first character in the second paragraph.

2 Press **+Backspace** until the paragraphs are joined.

39

INSERT TEXT

In the Insert mode, the text you type appears at the current insertion point location. Any existing text moves forward to make room for the new text.

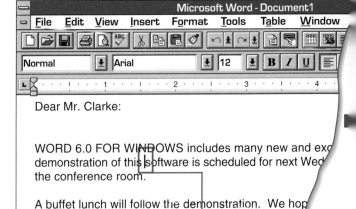

Microsoft Word - Document1

File   Edit   View   Insert   Format   Tools   Table   Window

Normal   Arial   12   **B** *I* U

Dear Mr. Clarke:

WORD 6.0 FOR WINDOWS includes many new and exc demonstration of this software is scheduled for next Wed the conference room.

A buffet lunch will follow the demonstration. We hop

Yours truly,

When you start Word, the program is in the Insert mode.

1 Position the insertion point where you want to insert the new text.

*Note: If the letters **OVR** appear in black (OVR) at the bottom of your screen, press **Insert** on your keyboard to switch to the **Insert** mode.*

40

This sentence moves forward as you type.

------------------------This sentence moves forward as you type.

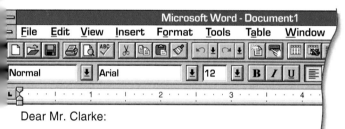

Microsoft Word - Document1

File   Edit   View   Insert   Format   Tools   Table   Window

Normal   Arial   12   **B** *I* U

Dear Mr. Clarke:

WORD 6.0 FOR WINDOWS includes many new and exc
demonstration of this latest software is scheduled for nex
a.m. in the conference room.

A buffet lunch will follow the demonstration. We hop

Yours truly,

Type the text you want insert (example: **latest**).

To insert a blank space, ess the **Spacebar**.

Note: The words to the right of the inserted text are pushed forward.

OVERTYPE TEXT

In the Overtype mode, the text you type appears at the current insertion point location. The new text replaces (types over) any existing text.

OVERTYPE TEXT

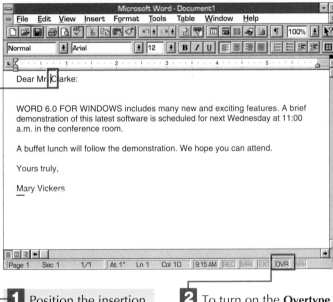

1 Position the insertion point to the left of the first character you want to replace.

2 To turn on the **Overtype** mode, move the mouse over OVR and then quickly press the left button twice (OVR changes to OVR).

42

This sentence disappears as you type.

xxxxxxxxxxxxxxxxxxxpears as you type.

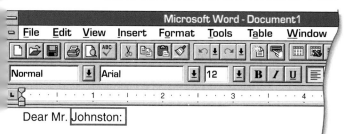

Microsoft Word - Document1

File   Edit   View   Insert   Format   Tools   Table   Window

Normal   Arial   12   B I U

Dear Mr. Johnston:

WORD 6.0 FOR WINDOWS includes many new and ex
demonstration of this latest software is scheduled for ne
a.m. in the conference room.

A buffet lunch will follow the demonstration. We hop

Yours truly,

3 Type the text you want
to replace the existing text
with (example: **Johnston:**).

*Note: The new text types over the
existing text.*

4 To turn off the **Overtype**
mode, repeat step **2**
(OVR changes to OVR).

Note: You can also press **Insert** *on
your keyboard to turn on or off the
Overtype mode.*

DELETE A BLANK LINE

You can use Delete to remove the blank line the insertion point is on. The remaining text moves up one line.

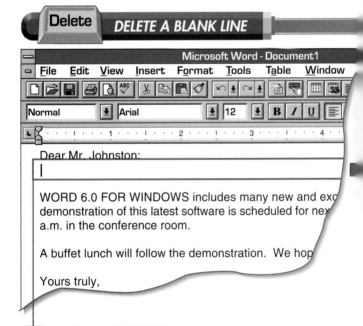

Microsoft Word - Document1

File   Edit   View   Insert   Format   Tools   Table   Window

Normal   Arial   12   B   I   U

Dear Mr. Johnston:

|

WORD 6.0 FOR WINDOWS includes many new and exc
demonstration of this latest software is scheduled for nex
a.m. in the conference room.

A buffet lunch will follow the demonstration. We hop

Yours truly,

1 Position the insertion point at the beginning of the blank line you want to delete.

44

Mr. Johnston:

> FOR WINDOWS includes many new and exciting features. A brief
ration of this latest software is scheduled for next Wednesday at 11:00
e conference room.

nch will follow the demonstration. We hope you can attend.

s

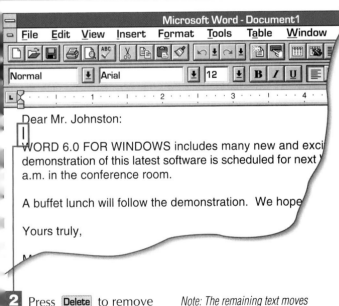

Microsoft Word - Document1

File   Edit   View   Insert   Format   Tools   Table   Window

Normal   Arial   12   **B** *I* U

Dear Mr. Johnston:

WORD 6.0 FOR WINDOWS includes many new and exci
demonstration of this latest software is scheduled for next
a.m. in the conference room.

A buffet lunch will follow the demonstration. We hope

Yours truly,

M

2 Press Delete to remove   *Note: The remaining text moves*
the blank line.   *up one line.*

DELETE A CHARACTER

You can use Delete to remove the character to the right of the insertion point. The remaining text moves to the left.

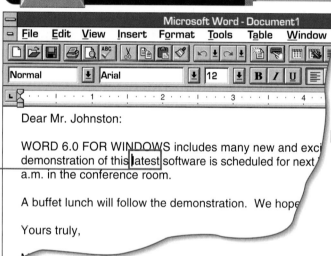

Delete — DELETE A CHARACTER

Microsoft Word - Document1

File   Edit   View   Insert   Format   Tools   Table   Window

Normal   Arial   12   B   I   U

Dear Mr. Johnston:

WORD 6.0 FOR WINDOWS includes many new and exci demonstration of this latest software is scheduled for next a.m. in the conference room.

A buffet lunch will follow the demonstration. We hope

Yours truly,

1 Position the insertion point to the left of the character you want to delete (example: l in latest).

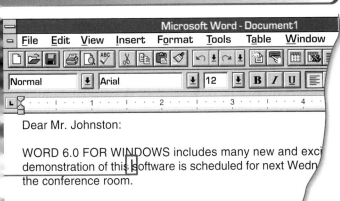

Dear Mr. Johnston:

WORD 6.0 FOR WINDOWS includes many new and exci
demonstration of this software is scheduled for next Wedn
the conference room.

A buffet lunch will follow the demonstration. We hope

Yours truly,

2 Press **Delete** once for each character you want to delete (example: press **Delete** seven times).

You can also use this key to delete characters. Position the insertion point to the right of the character(s) you want to delete and then press **◄Backspace**.

DELETE SELECTED TEXT

Delete DELETE SELECTED TEXT

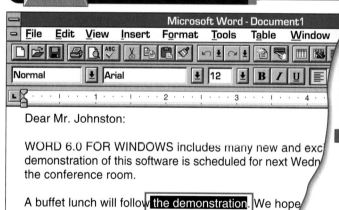

1 Select the text you want to delete.

Note: To select text, refer to pages 28 to 31.

You can use Delete to remove text you have selected. The remaining text moves up or to the left.

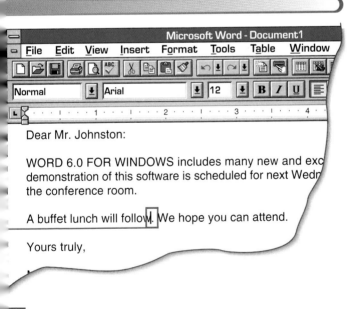

Microsoft Word - Document1

File   Edit   View   Insert   Format   Tools   Table   Window

Normal   Arial   12   B   I   U

Dear Mr. Johnston:

WORD 6.0 FOR WINDOWS includes many new and exc
demonstration of this software is scheduled for next Wedn
the conference room.

A buffet lunch will follow. We hope you can attend.

Yours truly,

2 Press Delete to remove the text.

UNDO CHANGES

Word remembers the last 100 changes you made to your document. If you regret these changes, you can cancel them by using the Undo feature.

UNDO CHANGES

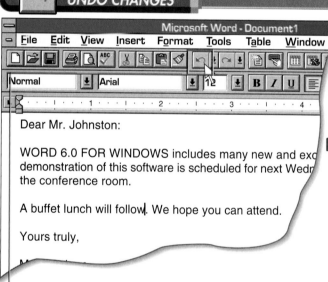

Microsoft Word - Document1

File   Edit   View   Insert   Format   Tools   Table   Window

Normal   Arial   12   **B** *I* U

Dear Mr. Johnston:

WORD 6.0 FOR WINDOWS includes many new and exc
demonstration of this software is scheduled for next Wedr
the conference room.

A buffet lunch will follow. We hope you can attend.

Yours truly,

1 To cancel the last change you made to your document, move the mouse � over 🔄 and then press the left button.

50

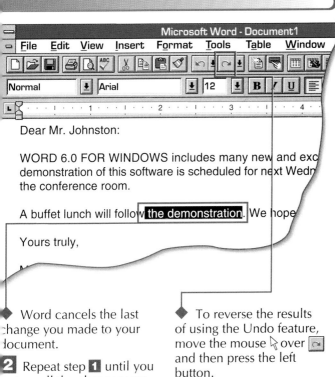

Dear Mr. Johnston:

WORD 6.0 FOR WINDOWS includes many new and exc
demonstration of this software is scheduled for next Wedn
the conference room.

A buffet lunch will follow the demonstration. We hope

Yours truly,

◆ Word cancels the last change you made to your document.

2 Repeat step **1** until you restore all the changes you regret.

◆ To reverse the results of using the Undo feature, move the mouse ⇦ over 🔁 and then press the left button.

51

MOVE TEXT

DRAG AND DROP TEXT

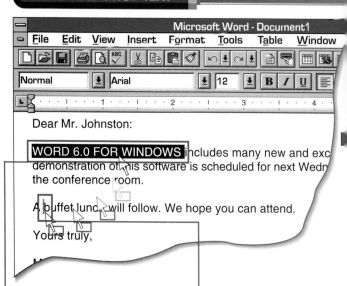

Microsoft Word - Document1

File   Edit   View   Insert   Format   Tools   Table   Window

Normal   Arial   12   B I U

Dear Mr. Johnston:

WORD 6.0 FOR WINDOWS includes many new and exc
demonstration of this software is scheduled for next Wedn
the conference room.

A buffet lunch will follow. We hope you can attend.

Yours truly,

1 Select the text you want to move.

2 Move the mouse I anywhere over the selected text (I becomes ↘).

3 Press and hold down the left button (↘ becomes 🖑).

4 Still holding down the le button, move the mouse 🖑 where you want to place the text.

Note: The text will appear where you position the dotted insertion point on your screen.

52

You can use the Drag and Drop feature to move text from one ocation in your document to another. The original text disappears.

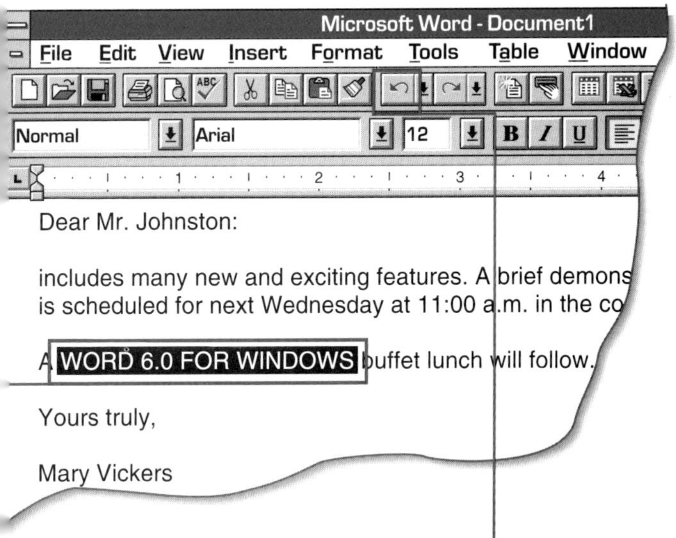
Microsoft Word - Document1
File Edit View Insert Format Tools Table Window
Normal
Arial
12
Dear Mr. Johnston:
includes many new and exciting features. A brief demons
is scheduled for next Wednesday at 11:00 a.m. in the co
A WORD 6.0 FOR WINDOWS buffet lunch will follow.
Yours truly,
Mary Vickers

5 Release the button nd the text moves to ıe new location.

CANCEL THE MOVE

◆ To immediately cancel the move, position the mouse over ↶ and then press the left button.

MOVE TEXT

CUT AND PASTE TEXT

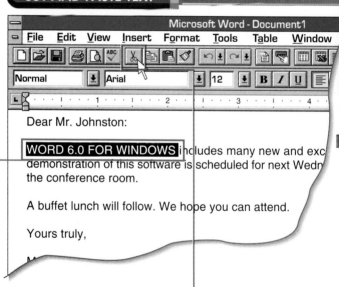

Microsoft Word - Document1

File   Edit   View   Insert   Format   Tools   Table   Window

Normal   Arial   12   B   I   U

Dear Mr. Johnston:

WORD 6.0 FOR WINDOWS includes many new and exc
demonstration of this software is scheduled for next Wedn
the conference room.

A buffet lunch will follow. We hope you can attend.

Yours truly,

1 Select the text you want to move.

2 Move the mouse over ✂ and then press the left button. The text you selected disappears from your screen.

54

The Cut and Paste features let you move text from one location in your document to another. The original text disappears.

```
 ─                          Microsoft Word - Document1
 ─   File   Edit   View   Insert   Format   Tools   Table   Window
 [D][🖙][🖫][🖨][🔍][ABC]   [✂][🖺][🖊]   [↶↓][↷↓]   [🖹][🗐]   [🎞][🖼]
 [Normal      ⬇][Arial              ⬇][12 ⬇][B][I][U][≣]
 L[🖟]····│····1····│····2····│····│····3····│····│····4·
```

Dear Mr. Johnston:

includes many new and exciting features. A brief demons
is scheduled for next Wednesday at 11:00 a.m. in the co

A WORD 6.0 FOR WINDOWS buffet lunch will follow.

Yours truly,

Mary Vickers

3 Position the insertion point where you want to move the text.

4 Move the mouse ↖ over 🖺 and then press the left button.

◆ The text appears in the new location.

COPY TEXT

You can use the Drag and Drop feature to copy text from one location in your document to another. The original text remains in its place.

DRAG AND DROP TEXT

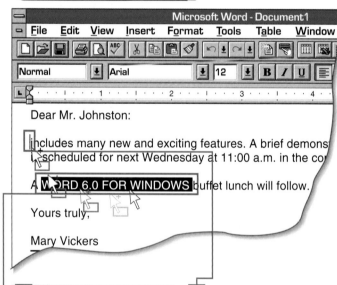

Microsoft Word - Document1

File Edit View Insert Format Tools Table Window

Normal   Arial   12   B I U

Dear Mr. Johnston:

ncludes many new and exciting features. A brief demons
scheduled for next Wednesday at 11:00 a.m. in the co

A WORD 6.0 FOR WINDOWS buffet lunch will follow.

Yours truly,

Mary Vickers

1 Select the text you want to copy.

2 Move the mouse I anywhere over the selected text (I becomes ↘).

3 Press and hold down Ctrl and press and hold down the left button (↘ becomes ↘).

4 Still holding down Ctrl and the left button, drag the mouse ↖ where you want to place the copy.

Note: The text will appear where you position the dotted insertion point on your screen.

56

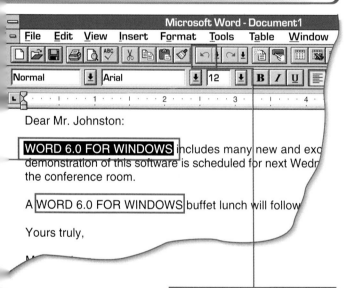

Dear Mr. Johnston:

WORD 6.0 FOR WINDOWS includes many new and exc
demonstration of this software is scheduled for next Wedn
the conference room.

A WORD 6.0 FOR WINDOWS buffet lunch will follow

Yours truly,

5 Release the button
and then Ctrl .

◆ A copy of the text
appears in the new
location.

CANCEL THE COPY

◆ To immediately
cancel the copy, position
the mouse ⇩ over 🔄 and
then press the left button.

COPY TEXT

The Copy and Paste features let you copy text from one location in your document to another. The original text remains in its place.

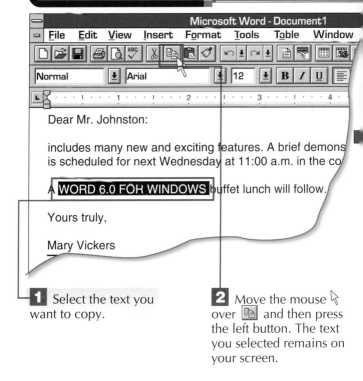

Dear Mr. Johnston:

includes many new and exciting features. A brief demons is scheduled for next Wednesday at 11:00 a.m. in the co

A WORD 6.0 FOR WINDOWS buffet lunch will follow.

Yours truly,

Mary Vickers

1 Select the text you want to copy.

2 Move the mouse over and then press the left button. The text you selected remains on your screen.

58

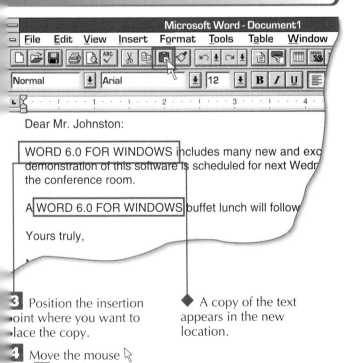

Dear Mr. Johnston:

WORD 6.0 FOR WINDOWS includes many new and exc
demonstration of this software is scheduled for next Wedr
the conference room.

A WORD 6.0 FOR WINDOWS buffet lunch will follow

Yours truly,

3 Position the insertion point where you want to place the copy.

4 Move the mouse ☐ over ☐ and then press the left button.

◆ A copy of the text appears in the new location.

CHANGE THE CASE OF TEXT

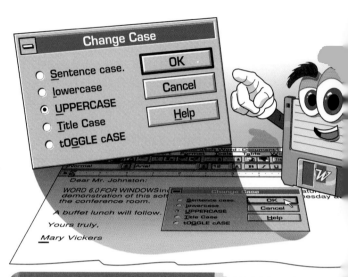

CHANGE THE CASE OF TEXT

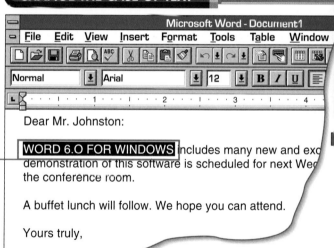

Dear Mr. Johnston:

WORD 6.O FOR WINDOWS includes many new and exc
demonstration of this software is scheduled for next Wed
the conference room.

A buffet lunch will follow. We hope you can attend.

Yours truly,

1 To change the case of text in your document, select the text you want to change.

Note: To select text, refer to pages 28 to 31.

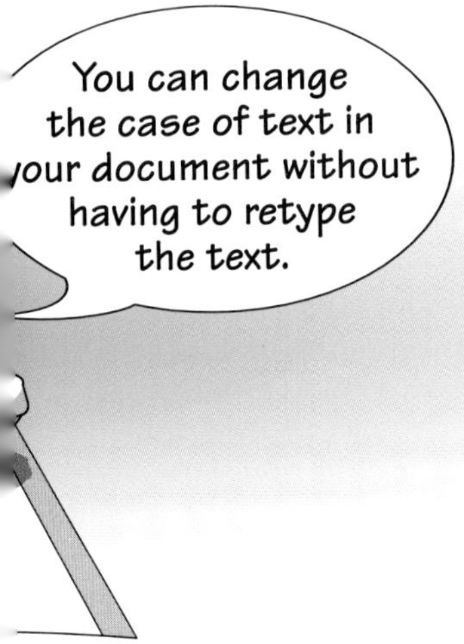
You can change the case of text in your document without having to retype the text.

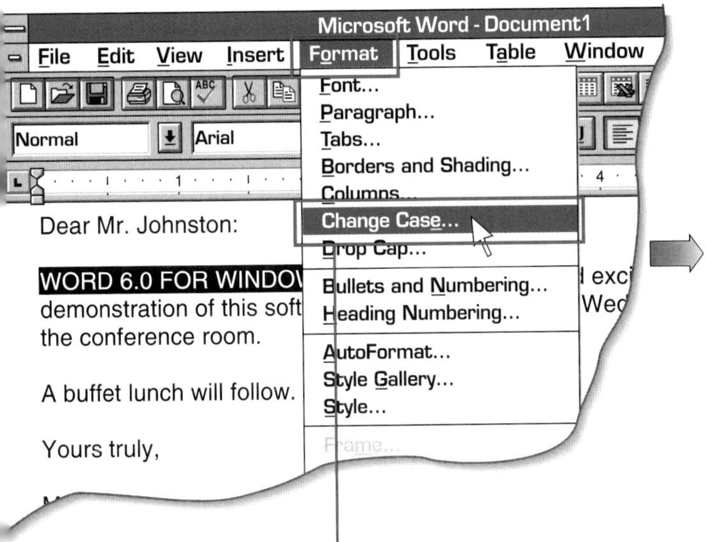
Microsoft Word - Document1
File Edit View Insert Format Tools Table Window
Normal
Arial
Font...
Paragraph...
Tabs...
Borders and Shading...
Columns...
Change Case...
Drop Cap...
Bullets and Numbering...
Heading Numbering...
AutoFormat...
Style Gallery...
Style...
Frame...
Dear Mr. Johnston:
WORD 6.0 FOR WINDO
demonstration of this soft
the conference room.
A buffet lunch will follow.
Yours truly,

2 Move the mouse over **Format** and then press the left button.

3 Move the mouse over **Change Case** and then press the left button.

Note: To continue, refer to the next page.

CHANGE THE CASE OF TEXT

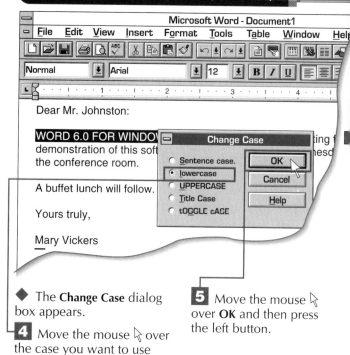

◆ The **Change Case** dialog box appears.

4 Move the mouse ⍉ over the case you want to use (example: **lowercase**) and then press the left button (O changes to ●).

5 Move the mouse ⍉ over **OK** and then press the left button.

62

Word offers
five case
options.

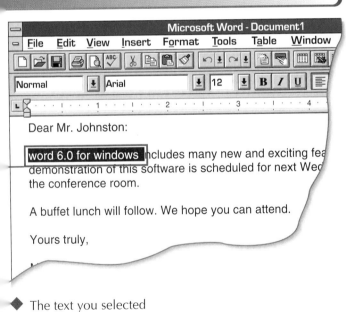

Microsoft Word - Document1

File   Edit   View   Insert   Format   Tools   Table   Window

Normal   Arial   12   **B** *I* U

Dear Mr. Johnston:

word 6.0 for windows includes many new and exciting fea
demonstration of this software is scheduled for next Wed
the conference room.

A buffet lunch will follow. We hope you can attend.

Yours truly,

◆ The text you selected
changes to the new case.

FIND TEXT

You can use the Find feature to locate a word or phrase in your document.

FIND TEXT

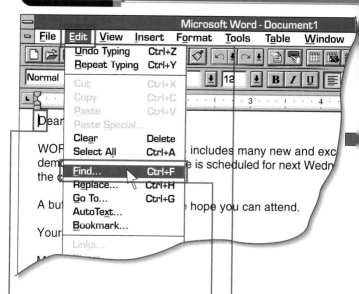

◆ Word searches your entire document, starting at the insertion point.

Note: To search only a section of your document, select the text before performing step 1. To select text, refer to pages 28 to 31.

1 Move the mouse ⌖ over **Edit** and then press the left button.

2 Move the mouse ⌖ over **Find** and then press the left button.

64

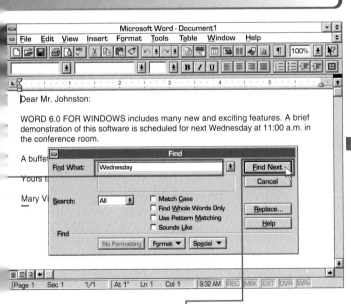

◆ The **Find** dialog box appears.

3 Type the text you want to find (example: **Wednesday**).

4 To find the next matching word in your document, move the mouse ⌕ over **Find Next** and then press the left button.

Note: To continue, refer to the next page.

FIND TEXT

You can cancel a search at any time by pressing **Esc**.

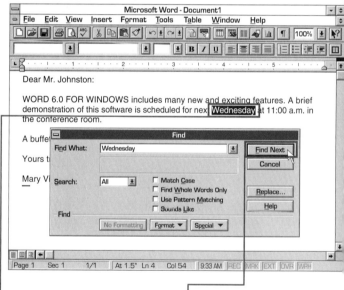

◆ Word highlights the first matching word it finds.

5 To find the next matching word, move the mouse ⬉ over **Find Next** and then press the left button.

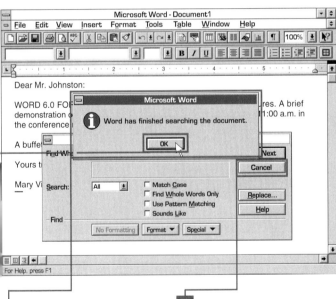

◆ This dialog box appears when there are no more matching words in your document.

6 To close the dialog box, move the mouse ⬚ over **OK** and then press the left button.

7 To close the **Find** dialog box, move the mouse ⬚ over **Cancel** and then press the left button.

REPLACE TEXT

Well Andrew, I was not surprised that you didn't win that **Nobel** prize thingy for chemistry. I mean honestly, who could possibly be doing anything more important in chemistry than you, and your subzero activated bug spray.

Obviously these **Nobel** types don't have any major bug problems. I refuse to believe that Europeans don't want a better bug spray, especially the more northern countries. And where do the **Nobel** prizes come from anyway - Switzerland! They probably have lots of uses for a subzero repellent in the Alps, but they're probably so busy swatting blackflies, they can't make a rational choice.

Send them a free sample, and you'll get the **Noble** prize next year...

REPLACE TEXT

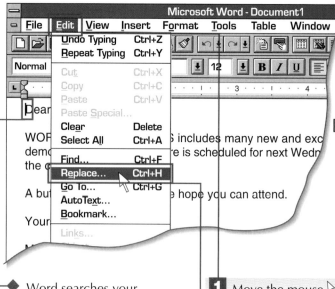

◆ Word searches your entire document, starting at the insertion point.

Note: To search only a section of your document, select the text before performing step **1**. *To select text, refer to pages 28 to 31.*

1 Move the mouse ⌖ over **Edit** and then press the left button.

2 Move the mouse ⌖ over **Replace** and then press the left button.

68

You can use the Replace feature to locate and replace every occurrence of a word or phrase in your document.

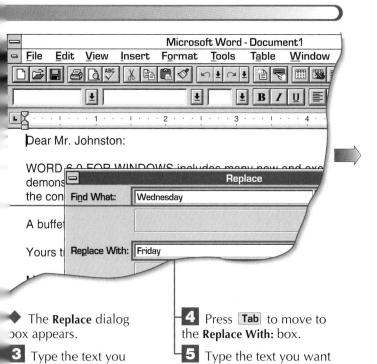

Microsoft Word - Document1

File　Edit　View　Insert　Format　Tools　Table　Window

Dear Mr. Johnston:

WORD 6.0 FOR WINDOWS includes many new and exc
demons
the con

Replace

Find What: Wednesday

A buffe

Yours t | Replace With: Friday

◆ The **Replace** dialog box appears.

3 Type the text you want to find (example: **Wednesday**).

4 Press **Tab** to move to the **Replace With:** box.

5 Type the text you want to replace the searched text with (example: **Friday**).

Note: To continue, refer to the next page.

69

REPLACE TEXT

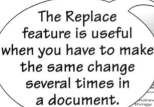

The Replace feature is useful when you have to make the same change several times in a document.

...ndrew, I ... ...urprised that you didn't win the **Nobel** thingy for chem... ... I mean honestly, who could possibly be ...g anything more ...portant in chemistry than you, and your ...ubzero activated bu...spray.

Obviously these **Nobel** ypes don't have any major bug problems. I refuse to believe that Europeans don't want a better bug spray, especially the more northern countries. And where do the **Nobel** prizes come from anyway - Switzerland! They probably have lots of uses for a subzero repellent in the Alps, but they're probably so busy swatting blackflies, they can't make a rational choice.

Send them a free sample, and you'll get the **Noble** prize next year...

REPLACE TEXT (Continued)

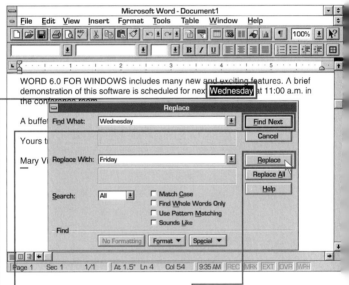

6 To start the search, move the mouse ⬚ over **Find Next** and then press the left button.

◆ Word highlights the first matching word it finds.

7 To replace the word, move the mouse ⬚ over **Replace** and then press the left button.

Note: If you do not want to replace the word, repeat step **6** to find the next matching word in your document.

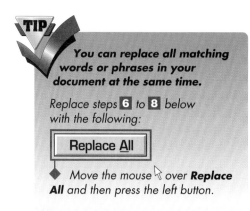

TIP

You can replace all matching words or phrases in your document at the same time.

Replace steps **6** to **8** below with the following:

Replace All

◆ Move the mouse � over **Replace All** and then press the left button.

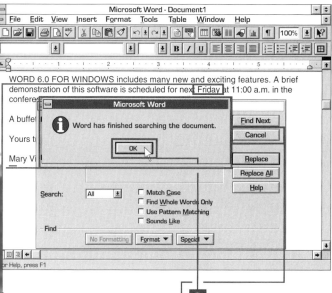

◆ Word replaces the word and searches for the next matching word.

8 Repeat step **7** for each word you want to replace.

◆ This dialog box appears when there are no more matching words in your document.

9 To close this dialog box, move the mouse � over **OK** and then press the left button.

10 To close the **Replace** dialog box, move the mouse � over **Cancel** or **Close** and then press the left button.

CHECK SPELLING

You can use the Spelling feature to find and correct spelling errors in your document.

Word Dictionary

 CHECK SPELLING

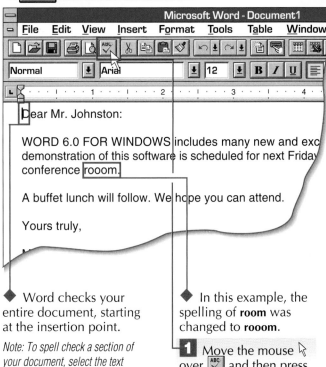

Microsoft Word - Document1

File   Edit   View   Insert   Format   Tools   Table   Window

Normal   Arial   12   **B** *I* U

Dear Mr. Johnston:

WORD 6.0 FOR WINDOWS includes many new and exc
demonstration of this software is scheduled for next Frida
conference rooom.

A buffet lunch will follow. We hope you can attend.

Yours truly,

◆ Word checks your entire document, starting at the insertion point.

Note: To spell check a section of your document, select the text before performing step **1** *. To select text, refer to pages 28 to 31.*

◆ In this example, the spelling of **room** was changed to **rooom**.

1 Move the mouse over and then press the left button.

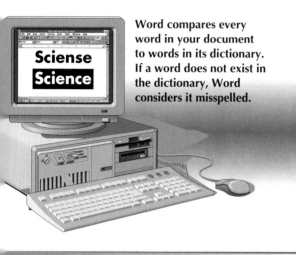

Word compares every word in your document to words in its dictionary. If a word does not exist in the dictionary, Word considers it misspelled.

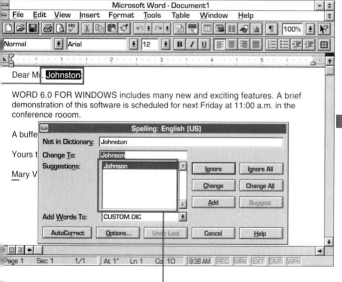

◆ The **Spelling** dialog box appears.

◆ Word highlights the first word it does not recognize (example: **Johnston**).

◆ The **Suggestions:** box displays alternative spellings.

Note: To continue, refer to the next page.

73

CHECK SPELLING

The Spell check will find many types of errors in your document.

Ignore misspelled word

2 If you do not want to change the spelling of the highlighted word, move the mouse ⌖ over **Ignore** and then press the left button.

Note: To change the spelling of a word and continue the spell check, refer to the next page.

74

The spell check will find:	Example:
Misspelled words	The girl is six **yeers** old.
Duplicate words	The girl is **six six** years old.

The spell check will not find:	Example:
A correctly spelled word used in the wrong context	The girl is **sit** years old.

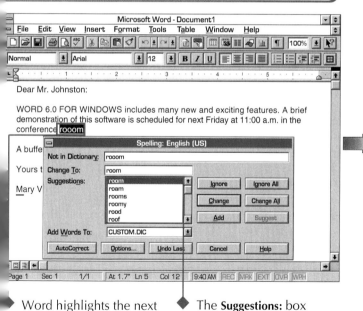

◆ Word highlights the next word it does not recognize (example: **rooom**).

◆ The **Suggestions:** box displays alternative spellings.

Note: To continue, refer to the next page.

CHECK SPELLING

CHECK SPELLING (Continued)

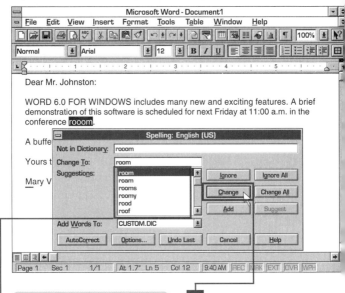

Correct misspelled word

3 To select the correct spelling, move the mouse ⌖ over the word you want to use (example: **room**) and then press the left button.

4 To replace the misspelle word in your document with the correct spelling, move th mouse ⌖ over **Change** and then press the left button.

To cancel the spell check at any time, move the mouse ⇞ over Close or Cancel and then press the left button.

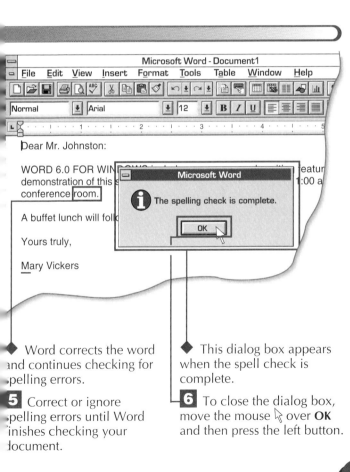

♦ Word corrects the word and continues checking for spelling errors.

5 Correct or ignore spelling errors until Word finishes checking your document.

♦ This dialog box appears when the spell check is complete.

6 To close the dialog box, move the mouse ⇞ over **OK** and then press the left button.

77

USING AUTOCORRECT

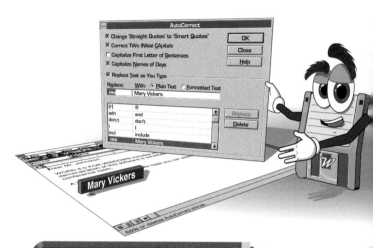

ADD TEXT TO AUTOCORRECT

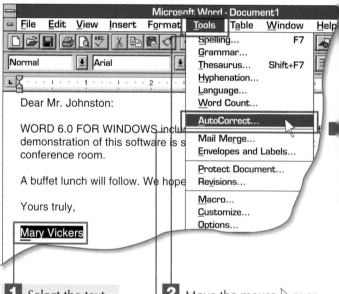

1 Select the text you want Word to automatically place in your documents.

Note: To select text, refer to pages 28 to 31.

2 Move the mouse ⬚ over **Tools** and then press the left button.

3 Move the mouse ⬚ over **AutoCorrect** and then press the left button.

Word automatically corrects common spelling errors as you type. You can customize the AutoCorrect list to include words you often misspell or words you frequently use.

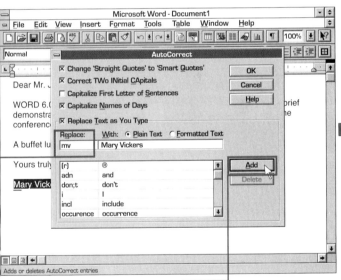

◆ The **AutoCorrect** dialog box appears.

4 Type the text you want Word to automatically replace every time you type it in a document (example: **mv**).

Note: This text cannot contain any spaces. Also, do not use a real word.

5 Move the mouse ⬚ over **Add** and then press the left button.

Note: To continue, refer to the next page.

79

USING AUTOCORRECT

If you type one of the following words and then press the Spacebar, Word will automatically change the word for you.

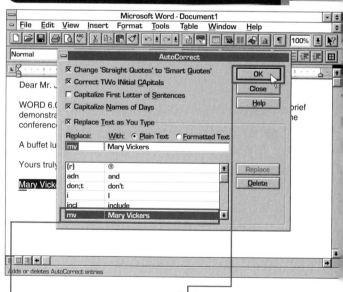

◆ The entry appears in the AutoCorrect list.

6 To close the **AutoCorrect** dialog box and return to your document, move the mouse over **OK** and then press the left button.

Text You Type	Replace With
(r)	®
adn	and
don;t	don't
i	I
incl	include
occurence	occurrence
recieve	receive
seperate	separate
teh	the

USING AUTOCORRECT

After you add text to the AutoCorrect list, Word will automatically change the text each time you type it in your document.

mv ➤ **Mary Vickers**

1 Position the insertion point where you want the text to appear.

2 Type the text (example: **mv**).

3 Press the **Spacebar** and the AutoCorrect text replaces the text you typed.

*Note: The text will not change until you press the **Spacebar**.*

USING AUTOTEXT

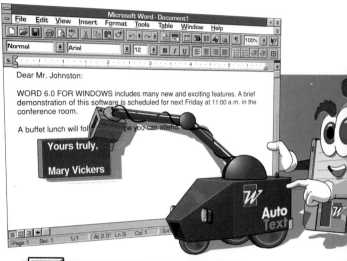

 ADD TEXT TO AUTOTEXT

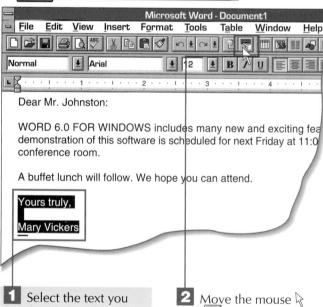

Dear Mr. Johnston:

WORD 6.0 FOR WINDOWS includes many new and exciting fea demonstration of this software is scheduled for next Friday at 11:0 conference room.

A buffet lunch will follow. We hope you can attend.

Yours truly,

Mary Vickers

1 Select the text you want to appear in your document each time you type its abbreviated name.

Note: To select text, refer to pages 28 to 31.

2 Move the mouse ⌖ over 📄 and then press the left button.

The AutoText feature lets you store frequently used words, phrases and sentences. You can then insert them into your document by typing an abbreviated version of the text.

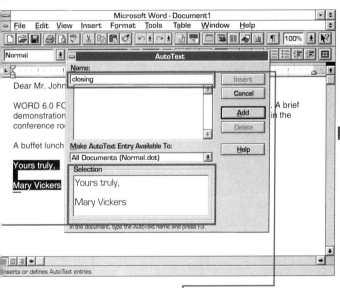

◆ The **AutoText** dialog box appears.

◆ The text you selected in your document appears in the **Selection** box.

3 Type an abbreviated name for the text (example: **closing**).

Note: To continue, refer to the next page.

83

USING AUTOTEXT

ADD TEXT TO AUTOTEXT (Continued)

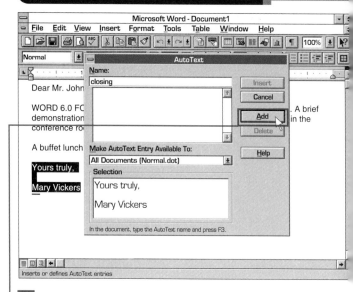

4 Move the mouse ⏳ over **Add** and then press the left button.

The AutoText and AutoCorrect features both insert text into your document. However, there are two distinct differences:

AUTOTEXT

◆ Use AutoText to insert groups of text or to insert text you use occasionally.

◆ Word inserts the text only when you instruct it to do so.

AUTOCORRECT

◆ Use AutoCorrect to correct your most common spelling errors or to insert text you use frequently (i.e., every day).

◆ Word automatically inserts the text as you type.

USING AUTOTEXT

After you add text to the AutoText list, you can insert the text into your document.

closing ➡ **Yours truly,**

Mary Vickers

1 Position the insertion point where you want the text to appear.

2 Type the name of the AutoText entry (example: **closing**).

3 Move the mouse ⌖ over 📰 and then press the left button.

◆ The AutoText entry replaces the text you typed in your document.

USING THE THESAURUS

The Thesaurus lets you replace a word in your document with one that is more suitable.

USING THE THESAURUS

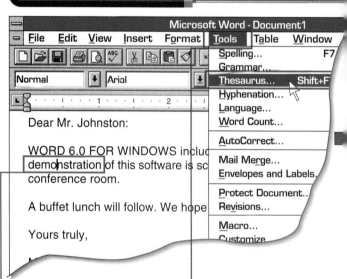

1 Move the mouse I anywhere over the word you want to look up (example: **demonstration**) and then press the left button.

2 Move the mouse ⤺ over **Tools** and then press the left button.

3 Move the mouse ⤺ over **Thesaurus** and then press the left button.

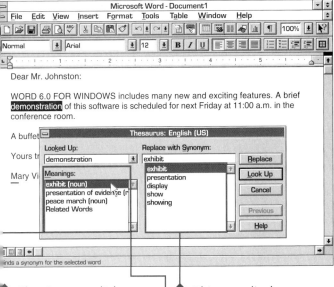

◆ The **Thesaurus** dialog box appears.

◆ This area displays different meanings for the word.

◆ This area displays alternative words for the highlighted meaning.

4 To display alternative words for another meaning, move the mouse ⌖ over the meaning and then press the left button.

Note: To continue, refer to the next page.

USING THE THESAURUS

You can use the Thesaurus to add variety to your writing.

USING THE THESAURUS (Continued)

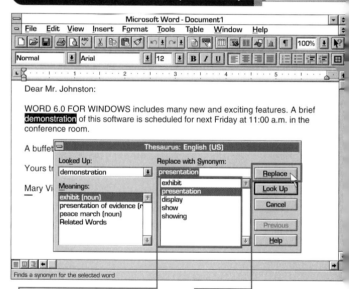

5 To select the word you want to use, move the mouse ⟋ over the word (example: **presentation**) and then press the left button.

6 Move the mouse ⟋ over **Replace** and then press the left button.

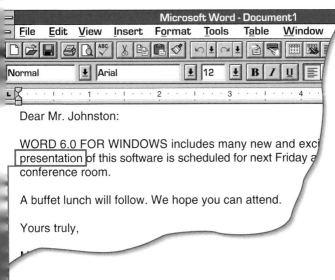

Dear Mr. Johnston:

WORD 6.0 FOR WINDOWS includes many new and exci
presentation of this software is scheduled for next Friday a
conference room.

A buffet lunch will follow. We hope you can attend.

Yours truly,

The word from the
hesaurus replaces the
/ord in your document.

DRIVES

Your computer stores programs and data in devices called "drives." Like a filing cabinet, a drive stores information in an organized way.

Drives

Most computers have one hard drive and one or two floppy drives to store information.

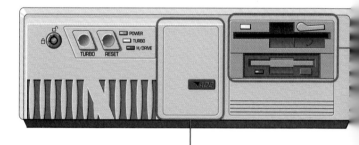

Hard drive (C:)

◆ A hard drive permanently stores programs and data. Most computers have at least one hard drive, called drive **C**.

*Note: Your computer may be set up to have additional hard drives (example: **drive D**).*

DRIVE NAME

A: ◆ A drive name consists of two parts: the letter and a colon (:). The colon represents the word "drive." For example, A: refers to the A drive.

Floppy drives (A: and B:)

◆ A floppy drive stores programs and data on removable diskettes (or floppy disks). A diskette operates slower and stores less data than a hard drive.

Diskettes are used to:
- Load new programs.
- Store backup copies of data.
- Transfer data to other computers.

If your computer has only one floppy drive, it is called drive A.

If your computer has two floppy drives, the second drive is called drive B.

DIRECTORIES

92

◆ Hard drive (C:)

A hard drive stores programs and data. It contains many directories to help organize your information.

◆ Files

When you save a document, Word stores it as a file.

◆ Directories

A directory usually contains related information. For example, the **winword** directory contains the Microsoft Word files.

When you save a document for the first time, you must give it a name.

A file name consists of two parts: a name and an extension. You must separate these parts with a period.

notice . doc

◆ **Name**

The name should describe the contents of a file. It can have up to eight characters.

◆ **Period**

A period must separate the name and the extension.

◆ **Extension**

The extension describes the type of information a file contains. It can have up to three characters.

Note: doc stands for document.

You should give your document a descriptive name to remind you of the information it contains.

A file name *can* contain the following characters:

◆ The letters A to Z, upper or lower case

◆ The numbers 0 to 9

◆ The symbols _ ^ $ ~ ! # % & { } @ ( )

A file name *cannot* contain the following characters:

◆ A comma (,)

◆ A blank space

◆ The symbols * ? ; [ ] + = \ / : < >

Each file in a directory must have a unique name.

letter.doc
note1q.doc
test.doc
training.doc

SAVE A NEW DOCUMENT

SAVE A NEW DOCUMENT

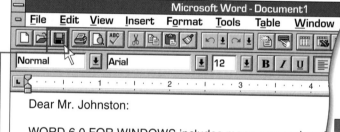

Microsoft Word - Document1

| File | Edit | View | Insert | Format | Tools | Table | Window |

Normal   Arial   12   **B** *I* U

Dear Mr. Johnston:

WORD 6.0 FOR WINDOWS includes many new and exci
presentation of this software is scheduled for next Friday
conference room.

A buffet lunch will follow. We hope you can attend.

Yours truly,

1 Move the mouse ⬚ over 💾 and then press the left button.

*Note: If you previously saved your document, the **Save As** dialog box will **not** appear since you have already named the file.*

96

You should save your document to store it for future use.

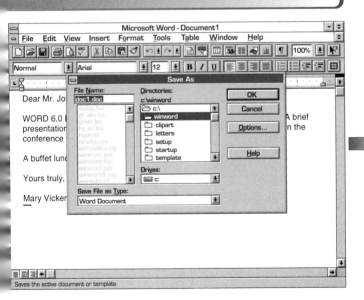

◆ The **Save As** dialog box appears.

Note: To continue, refer to the next page.

SAVE A NEW DOCUMENT

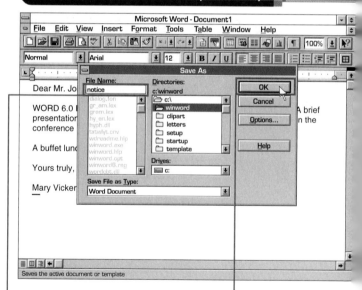

2 Type a name for your document (example: **notice**).

*Note: To make it easier to find your document later on, do not type an extension. Word will then automatically add the **doc** extension to the file name.*

3 Move the mouse over **OK** and then press the left button.

Saving a document enables you to later retrieve the document for reviewing or editing purposes.

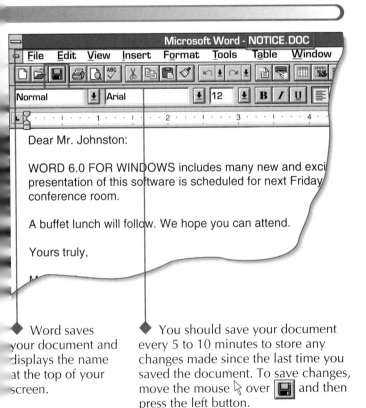

Microsoft Word - NOTICE.DOC

File   Edit   View   Insert   Format   Tools   Table   Window

Normal   Arial   12   B I U

Dear Mr. Johnston:

WORD 6.0 FOR WINDOWS includes many new and exci
presentation of this software is scheduled for next Friday
conference room.

A buffet lunch will follow. We hope you can attend.

Yours truly,

◆ Word saves your document and displays the name at the top of your screen.

◆ You should save your document every 5 to 10 minutes to store any changes made since the last time you saved the document. To save changes, move the mouse ⃝ over 🖫 and then press the left button.

SAVE A DOCUMENT TO A DISKETTE

SAVE A DOCUMENT TO A DISKETTE

MicroFLOPPY
Double Sided

Kari's Disk

1 Insert a diskette into a floppy drive (example: **drive a**).

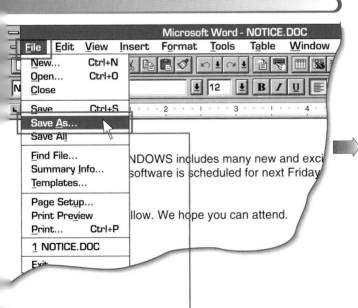

As a precaution, you should save your document to a diskette. You can then use this copy to replace any lost data if your hard drive fails or you accidentally erase the file.

2 Move the mouse � over **File** and then press the left button.

3 Move the mouse � over **Save As** and then press the left button.

Note: To continue, refer to the next page.

101

SAVE A DOCUMENT TO A DISKETTE

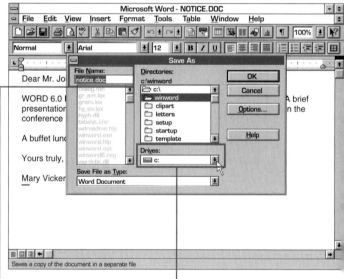

◆ The **Save As** dialog box appears.

◆ The **File Name:** box displays the current file name (example: **notice.doc**).

Note: To save your document with a different name, type a new name.

◆ The **Drives:** box displays the current drive (example: **c:**).

4 To save the file to a different drive, move the mouse ⬚ over ⬇ in the **Drives:** box and then press the left button.

You can transfer a file to another computer by saving your document to a diskette.

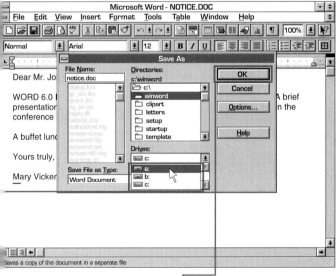

▶ A list of the available drives for your computer appears.

5 Move the mouse ↖ over the drive you want to use (example: **a:**) and then press the left button.

6 To save your document to the diskette, move the mouse ↖ over **OK** and then press the left button.

103

EXIT WORD

When you finish using Word, you can exit the program to return to the Windows Program Manager.

EXIT WORD

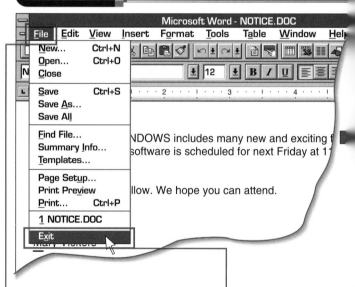

1 To exit Word, move the mouse ⌖ over **File** and then press the left button.

2 Move the mouse ⌖ over **Exit** and then press the left button.

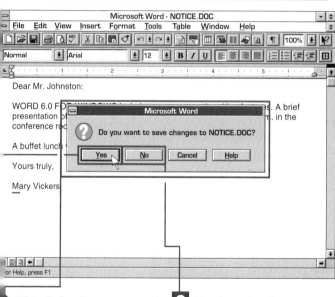

Microsoft Word - NOTICE.DOC

File   Edit   View   Insert   Format   Tools   Table   Window   Help

Normal   Arial   12   **B** *I* U

Dear Mr. Johnston:

WORD 6.0 F   WINDOWS   A brief
presentation   in the
conference r   Do you want to save changes to NOTICE.DOC?

A buffet lunch   Yes   No   Cancel   Help

Yours truly,

Mary Vickers

or Help, press F1

■ This dialog box appears if you have not saved changes made to your document.

■ To save changes, move the mouse ⬚ over **Yes** and then press the left button.

Note: For more information on saving a document, refer to page 96.

3 To close the document without saving the changes, move the mouse ⬚ over **No** and then press the left button.

OPEN A DOCUMENT

You can open a saved document and display it on your screen.

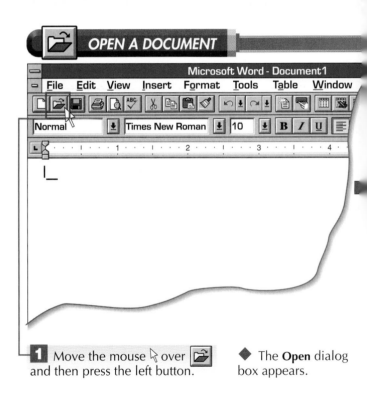

OPEN A DOCUMENT

1 Move the mouse ⬚ over 📂 and then press the left button.

◆ The **Open** dialog box appears.

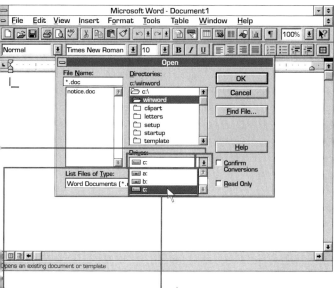

Opens an existing document or template

The **Drives:** box isplays the current drive example: **c:**).

2 To open a file on nother drive, move the nouse ▷ over ▣ in the **rives:** box and then press he left button.

◆ A list of the available drives for your computer appears.

3 Move the mouse ▷ over the drive containing the file you want to open and then press the left button.

Note: To continue, refer to the next page.

107

OPEN A DOCUMENT

> After you open a document, you can review and edit your work.

OPEN A DOCUMENT (Continued)

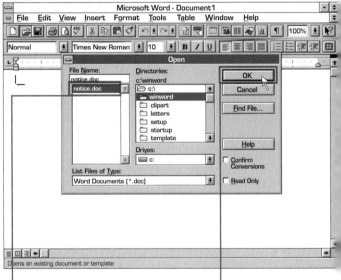

4 Move the mouse ⌖ over the name of the file you want to open (example: **notice.doc**) and then press the left button.

Note: If you cannot remember the name or location of the file you want to open, refer to page 110 to find the file.

5 Move the mouse ⌖ over **OK** and then press the left button.

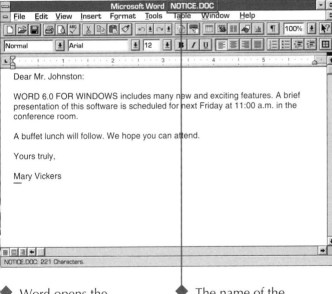

◆ Word opens the document and displays it on your screen. You can now make changes to the document.

◆ The name of the document appears at the top of your screen.

FIND A DOCUMENT

FIND A DOCUMENT

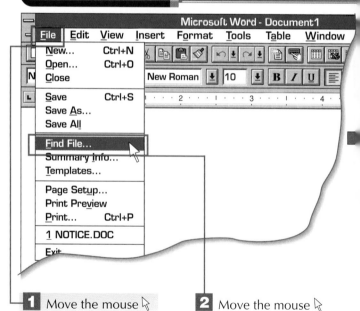

1 Move the mouse ⬚ over **File** and then press the left button.

2 Move the mouse ⬚ over **Find File** and then press the left button.

If you cannot remember the location of the document you want to open, you can use the Find File feature to search for the document.

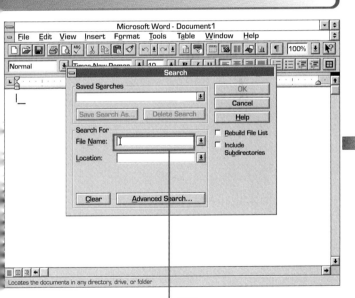

◆ The **Search** dialog box appears.

*Note: If the **Find File** dialog box appears, see IMPORTANT at the top of page 113.*

3 Move the mouse I over the box beside **File Name:** and then press the left button.

Note: To continue, refer to the next page.

FIND A DOCUMENT

FIND A DOCUMENT (Continued)

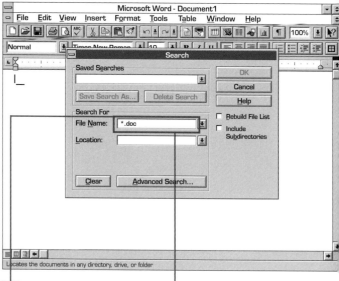

4 To search for a file with a particular extension, type ***.** followed by the extension. For example, type ***.doc** to find all files with the **doc** extension.

◆ To search for a file that begins with a particular sequence of letters, type the letters followed by the ***.*** characters. For example, type **n*.*** to find all files starting with **n**.

Important!

The Find File dialog box appears if you have previously used the Find File command. To display the Search dialog box and start a new search:

1 Move the `Search...` mouse over **Search** and then press the left button. The **Search** dialog box appears.

2 To clear `Clear` all the options you set for your last search, move the mouse over **Clear** and then press the left button.

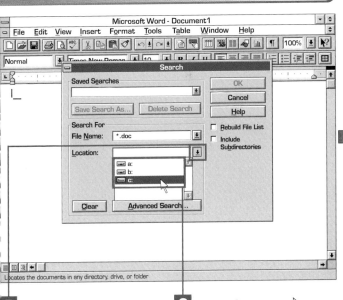

5 To select the drive you want to search, move the mouse over ⬇ beside the **Location:** box and then press the left button.

6 Move the mouse over the drive (example: **c:**) and then press the left button.

Note: To continue, refer to the next page.

FIND A DOCUMENT

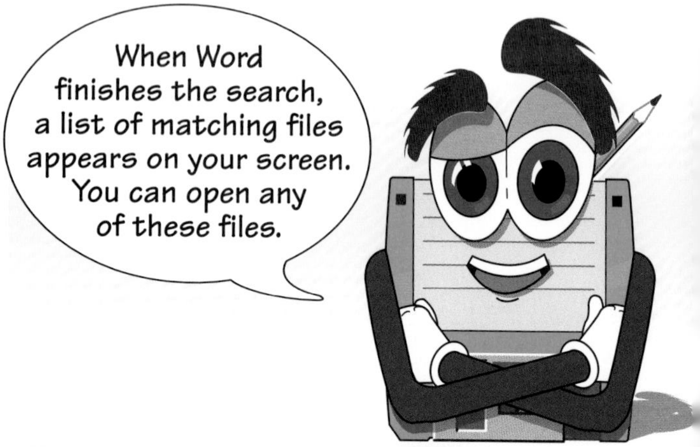
When Word finishes the search, a list of matching files appears on your screen. You can open any of these files.

FIND A DOCUMENT (Continued)

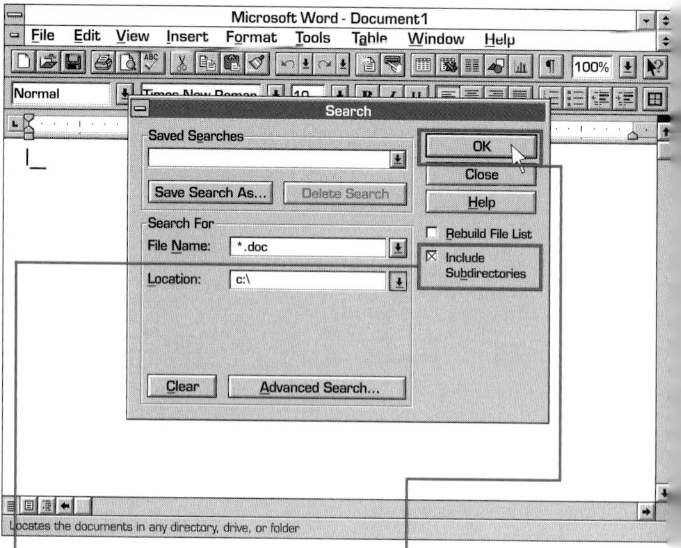
Microsoft Word - Document1
File Edit View Insert Format Tools Table Window Help
100%
Normal
Search
Saved Searches
Save Search As...
Delete Search
OK
Close
Help
Rebuild File List
Include Subdirectories
Search For
File Name: *.doc
Location: c:\
Clear
Advanced Search...
Locates the documents in any directory, drive, or folder

7 To search all subdirectories of the drive you selected, move the mouse ⇖ over **Include Subdirectories** and then press the left button (☐ changes to ☒).

8 To start the search, move the mouse ⇖ over **OK** and then press the left button.

TIP

To open a file displayed in the Find File dialog box:

1 Move the mouse ⌖ over the file name and then quickly press the left button twice.

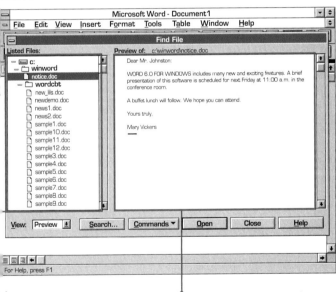

◆ After a few moments the **Find File** dialog box appears.

◆ This area displays the names of the files Word found.

◆ This area displays the contents of the highlighted file.

9 To display the contents of another file, press ↓ or ↑ on your keyboard.

CREATE A NEW DOCUMENT

You can create
a document to start
a new letter, report or
memo. Word lets you have
several documents open
at the same time.

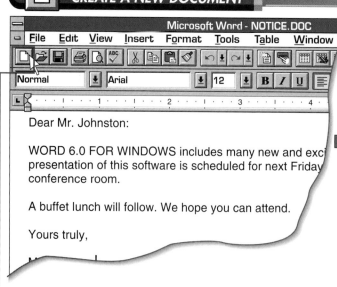

CREATE A NEW DOCUMENT

Microsoft Word - NOTICE.DOC

File   Edit   View   Insert   Format   Tools   Table   Window

Normal   Arial   12   B I U

Dear Mr. Johnston:

WORD 6.0 FOR WINDOWS includes many new and exci
presentation of this software is scheduled for next Friday
conference room.

A buffet lunch will follow. We hope you can attend.

Yours truly,

1 Move the mouse ⃗ over 🗋
and then press the left button.

116

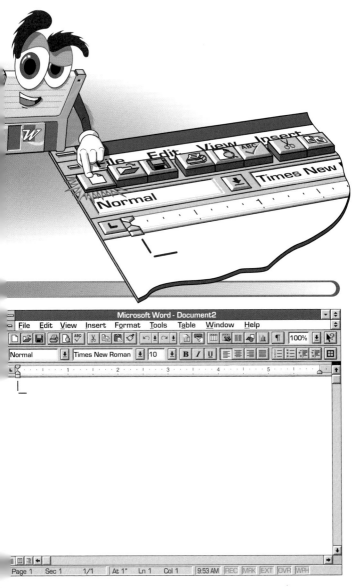

◆ A new document appears.

Note: The previous document is now hidden behind the new document.

◆ Think of each document as a separate piece of paper. When you create a document, you are placing a new piece of paper on your screen.

ARRANGE OPEN DOCUMENTS

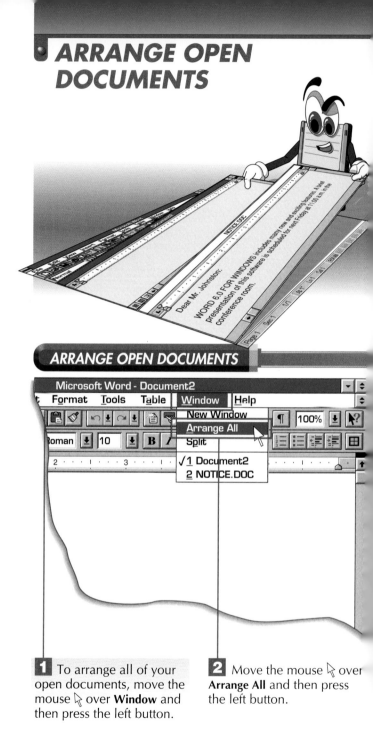

1 To arrange all of your open documents, move the mouse ▷ over **Window** and then press the left button.

2 Move the mouse ▷ over **Arrange All** and then press the left button.

118

If you have several documents open, some of them may be hidden from view. To view the contents of each document, you can use the Arrange All command.

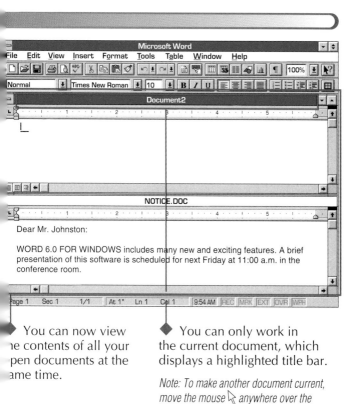

◆ You can now view the contents of all your open documents at the same time.

◆ You can only work in the current document, which displays a highlighted title bar.

Note: To make another document current, move the mouse ℝ anywhere over the document and then press the left button.

COPY OR MOVE TEXT BETWEEN DOCUMENTS

Copying or moving text between documents saves you time when you are working in one document and want to use text from another.

COPY OR MOVE TEXT BETWEEN DOCUMENTS

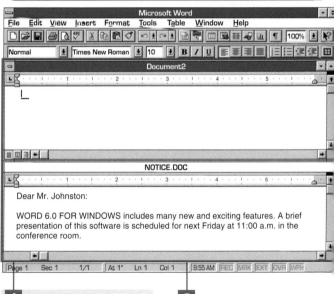

1 Open the documents you want to copy or move text between.

Note: To open a saved document, refer to page 106. To create a new document, refer to page 116.

2 Display the contents of both documents by using the **Arrange All** command.

*Note: For information on the **Arrange All** command, refer to page 118.*

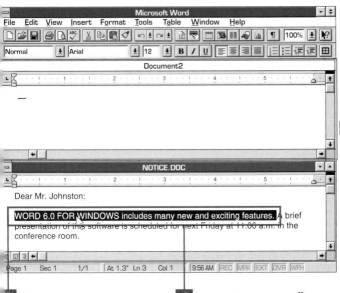

3 Select the text you want to copy or move to another document.

Note: To select text, refer to pages 28 to 31.

4 Move the mouse I anywhere over the selected text and I changes to ⬚.

Note: To continue, refer to the next page.

COPY OR MOVE TEXT BETWEEN DOCUMENTS

COPY OR MOVE TEXT (Continued)

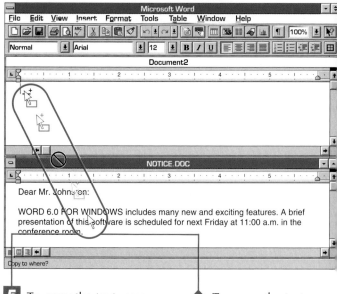

5 To copy the text, press and hold down `Ctrl`. Still holding down `Ctrl`, press and hold down the left button as you drag the mouse where you want to place the copy.

◆ To move the text, press and hold down the left button as you drag the mouse where you want to move the text.

122

COPY TEXT

When you copy text, Word *copies* the text and *pastes* the copy in a new location. The original text remains in its place.

MOVE TEXT

When you move text, Word *cuts* the text and *pastes* it in a new location. The original text disappears.

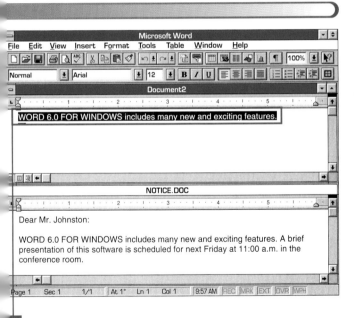

6 Release the button and the text appears in the new location.

MAXIMIZE A DOCUMENT

You can enlarge a document to fill your entire screen. This enables you to view more of its contents.

MAXIMIZE A DOCUMENT

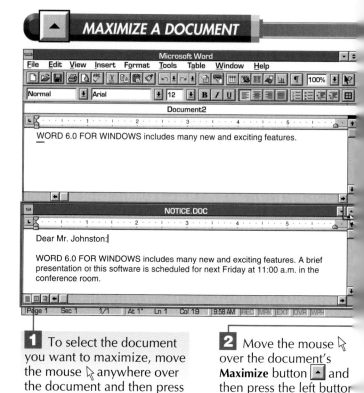

1 To select the document you want to maximize, move the mouse ⌖ anywhere over the document and then press the left button.

2 Move the mouse ⌖ over the document's **Maximize** button ▲ and then press the left button.

Dear Mr. Johnston:

WORD 6.0 FOR WINDOWS includes many new and exciting features. A brief
presentation of this software is scheduled for next Friday at 11:00 a.m. in the
conference room.

A buffet lunch will follow. We hope you can attend.

Yours truly,

Mary Vickers

◆ The document enlarges
o fill your entire screen.

*Note: The file you maximized covers
all of your open documents.*

SWITCH BETWEEN DOCUMENTS

You can easily switch between all of your open documents.

SWITCH BETWEEN DOCUMENTS

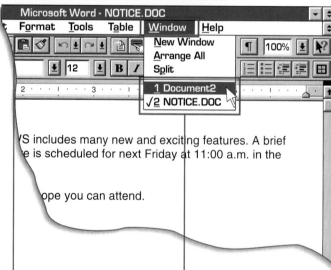

Microsoft Word - NOTICE.DOC

Format   Tools   Table   Window   Help

New Window
Arrange All
Split

1 Document2
√2 NOTICE.DOC

'S includes many new and exciting features. A brief
'e is scheduled for next Friday at 11:00 a.m. in the

ope you can attend.

1 To display a list of all your open documents, move the mouse ⇧ over **Window** and then press the left button.

2 Move the mouse ⇧ over the document you want to switch to and then press the left button.

◆ The document appears.

◆ Word displays the name of the document at the top of your screen.

CLOSE A DOCUMENT

When you finish working with a document, you can close the document.

CLOSE A DOCUMENT

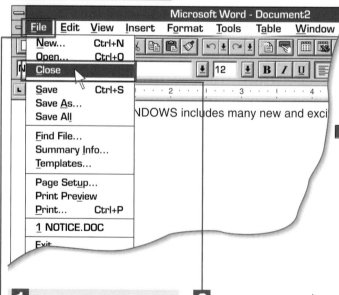

1 To close the document displayed on your screen, move the mouse ⇖ over **File** and then press the left button.

2 Move the mouse ⇖ over **Close** and then press the left button.

128

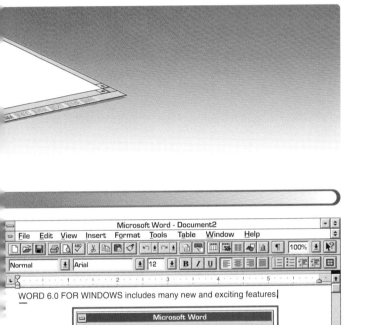

WORD 6.0 FOR WINDOWS includes many new and exciting features

Microsoft Word

(?) Do you want to save changes to Document2?

Yes   No   Cancel   Help

◆ This dialog box appears if you have not saved changes made to your document.

3 To close the document without saving the changes, move the mouse ⌖ over **No** and then press the left button.

◆ To save the changes, move the mouse ⌖ over **Yes** and then press the left button. For more information, refer to page 96.

Note: To continue, refer to the next page.

129

CLOSE A DOCUMENT

Closing a document removes it from your screen.

CLOSE A DOCUMENT (Continued)

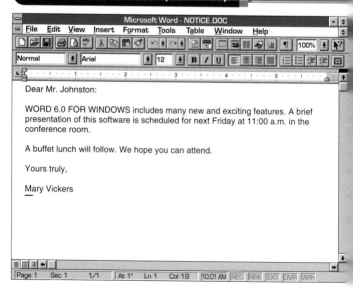

◆ Word removes the document from your screen.

Note: If you had more than one document open, the second last document you worked on appears.

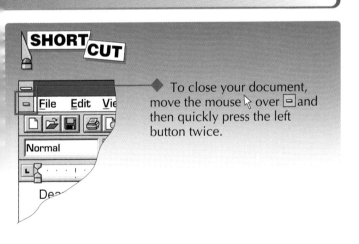

SHORT CUT

To close your document, move the mouse ⬚ over ⊟ and then quickly press the left button twice.

PREVIEW A DOCUMENT

PREVIEW A DOCUMENT

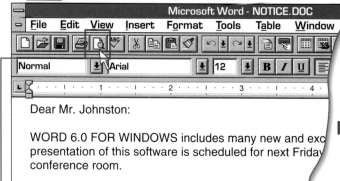

Dear Mr. Johnston:

WORD 6.0 FOR WINDOWS includes many new and exc
presentation of this software is scheduled for next Frida
conference room.

A buffet lunch will follow. We hope you can attend.

Yours truly,

1 Move the mouse ⬚ over ⬚
and then press the left button.

132

The Print Preview feature lets you see on screen what your document will look like when printed.

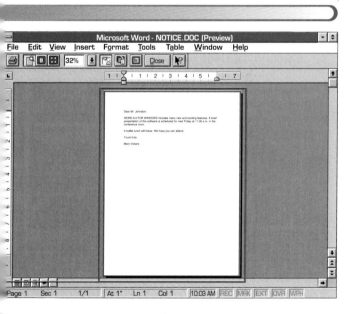

The page you are currently working on appears in the Print Preview window.

If your document contains more than one page, press **PageDown** on your keyboard to display the next page. Press **PageUp** to display the previous page.

PREVIEW A DOCUMENT

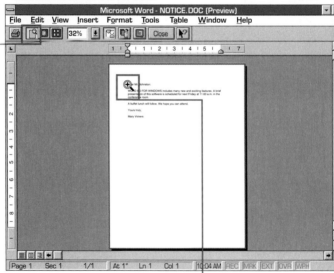

◆ If the mouse looks like I when over your document, you are in the editing mode.

1 To change to the zoom mode, move the mouse ↖ over ⬛ and then press the left button (I changes to ⊕).

2 To magnify a section of the page, move the mouse ⊕ over the section and then press the left button.

134

You can magnify a section of your document in Print Preview. This lets you make last minute changes before printing your document.

Note: To display your document in Print Preview, refer to page 132.

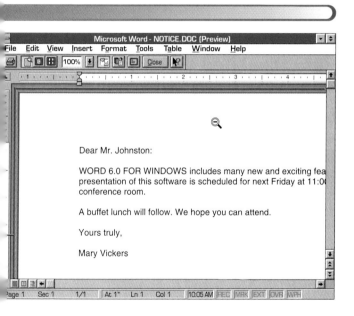

→ A magnified view of the page appears and the mouse ⊕ changes to ⊖.

Note: To switch to the editing mode, repeat step 1.

3 To again display the entire page, move the mouse ⊖ anywhere over the page and then press the left button.

PREVIEW A DOCUMENT

DISPLAY MULTIPLE PAGES

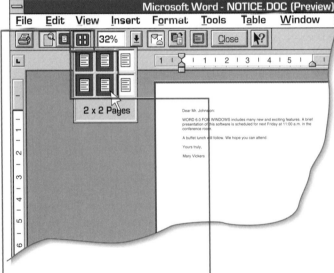

Microsoft Word - NOTICE.DOC (Preview)

File   Edit   View   Insert   Format   Tools   Table   Window   H

32%   Close

2 x 2 Pages

Dear Mr. Johnson:

WORD 6.0 FOR WINDOWS includes many new and exciting features. A brief presentation of this software is scheduled for next Friday at 11:00 a.m. in the conference room.

A buffet lunch will follow. We hope you can attend.

Yours truly,

Mary Vickers

1 Move the mouse ⬚ over ⊞ and then press and hold down the left button.

Note: To display your document in Print Preview, refer to page 132.

2 Still holding down th button, move the mouse over the number of page you want to display at once.

Note: If you drag the mouse ⬚ do or to the right, more options appe

In Print Preview,
Word can display more
than one page at a time.
This lets you view the overall
style of multiple pages
at once.

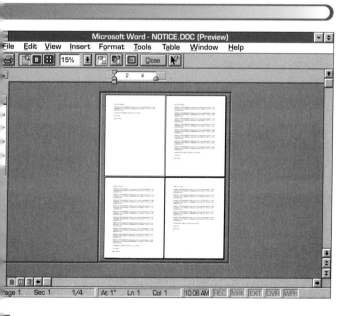

3 Release the button and
the number of pages you
specified appears on your
screen.

*Note: In this example, the document
contains four pages.*

PREVIEW A DOCUMENT

You can view one page at a time in the Print Preview window.

DISPLAY ONE PAGE

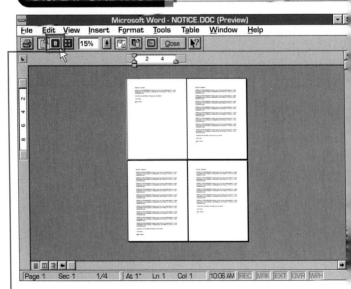

1 To display a single page, move the mouse ⍇ over ▤ and then press the left button.

Note: To display your document Print Preview, refer to page 132.

138

SHRINK TO FIT

If the last page in your document has only a few lines of text, you can have Word fit the text on the second last page. This will remove one page from your document.

1 Move the mouse ⬚ over 🖻 on the Print Preview toolbar and then press the left button.

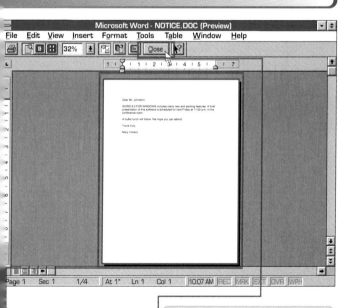

◆ A single page appears on your screen.

◆ Press **PageDown** on your keyboard to display the next page. Press **PageUp** to display the previous page.

Close Print Preview

1 To close Print Preview and return to your document, move the mouse ⬚ over **Close** and then press the left button.

139

PRINT A DOCUMENT

You can print a single page, specific pages or your entire document.

PRINT A DOCUMENT

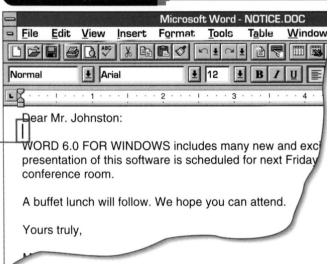

Microsoft Word - NOTICE.DOC

File   Edit   View   Insert   Format   Tools   Table   Window

Normal   Arial   12   B I U

Dear Mr. Johnston:

WORD 6.0 FOR WINDOWS includes many new and exci presentation of this software is scheduled for next Friday conference room.

A buffet lunch will follow. We hope you can attend.

Yours truly,

1 To print a single page, position the insertion point anywhere on the page you want to print.

◆ To print your entire document or specific pages, position the insertion point anywhere in the document.

◆ To print a small section of text, select the text.

Note: To select text, refer to pages 28 to 31.

140

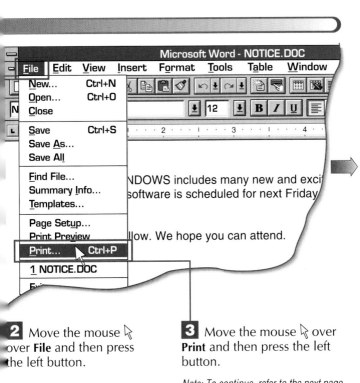

2 Move the mouse ⅓ over **File** and then press the left button.

3 Move the mouse ⅓ over **Print** and then press the left button.

Note: To continue, refer to the next page.

141

PRINT A DOCUMENT

Before printing your document, make sure your printer is on and it contains paper.

PRINT A DOCUMENT (Continued)

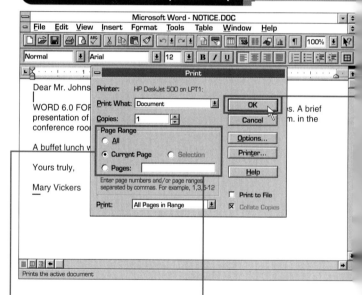

◆ The **Print** dialog box appears.

4 Move the mouse ⟍ over the range you want to print (example: **Current Page**) and then press the left button.

◆ To print specific pages in your document, select **Pages:** in step **4**. Then type the page numbers separated by commas (example: **1,3,5**) or type the first and last page numbers separated by a dash (example: **3-5**).

SHORT CUT

◆ To quickly print your entire document, move the mouse � over 🖨 and then press the left button.

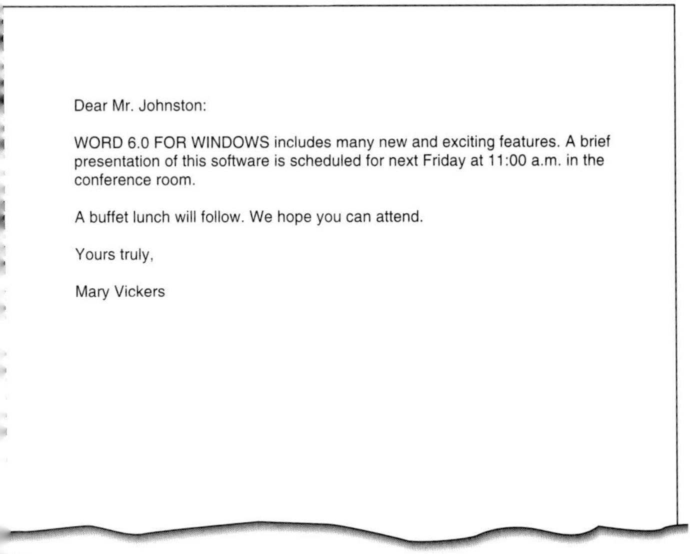

Dear Mr. Johnston:

WORD 6.0 FOR WINDOWS includes many new and exciting features. A brief presentation of this software is scheduled for next Friday at 11:00 a.m. in the conference room.

A buffet lunch will follow. We hope you can attend.

Yours truly,

Mary Vickers

---

5 To print your document, move the mouse � over **OK** and then press the left button.

CHANGE VIEWS

Word offers three basic views that you can use to display your document.

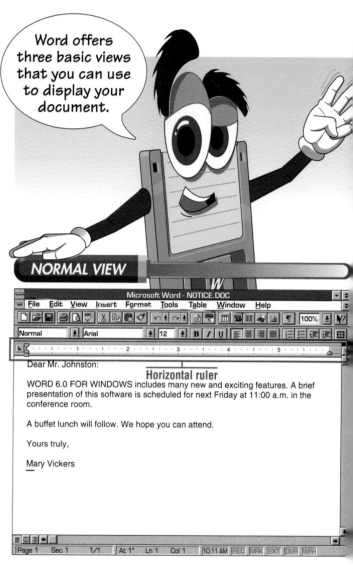

NORMAL VIEW

Microsoft Word - NOTICE.DOC

File   Edit   View   Insert   Format   Tools   Table   Window   Help

Normal   Arial   12   **B** *I* U

Horizontal ruler

Dear Mr. Johnston:

WORD 6.0 FOR WINDOWS includes many new and exciting features. A brief presentation of this software is scheduled for next Friday at 11:00 a.m. in the conference room.

A buffet lunch will follow. We hope you can attend.

Yours truly,

Mary Vickers

Page 1   Sec 1   1/1   At 1"   Ln 1   Col 1   10:11 AM   REC   MRK   EXT   OVR   WPH

◆ The Normal view simplifies the page layout so you can type and edit the document quickly.

◆ This view does not display top or bottom margins, headers, footers or page numbers.

OUTLINE VIEW

◆ The Outline view lets you create an outline of your document, similar to a Table of Contents. You can display the headings and subheadings and hide the body text. This view helps you work more efficiently with longer documents.

PAGE LAYOUT VIEW

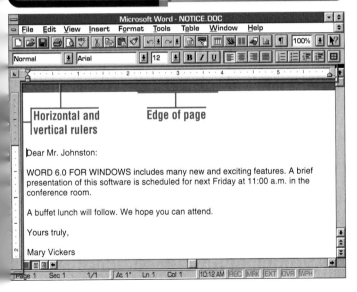

◆ The Page Layout view displays your document exactly the way it will appear on a printed page.

◆ This view displays all features in your document including top and bottom margins, headers, footers and page numbers.

145

CHANGE VIEWS

You can select a different view at any time to better suit your needs.

CHANGE VIEWS

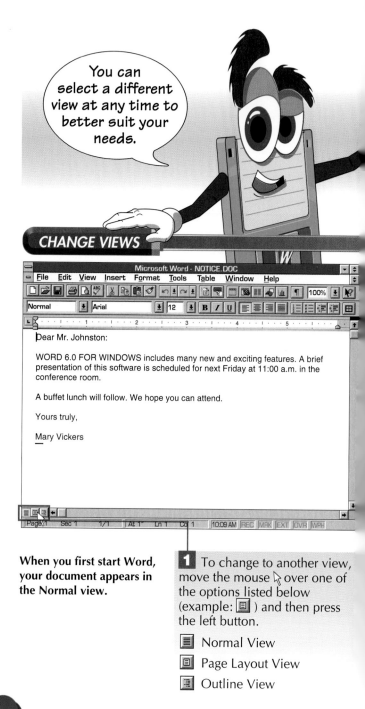

When you first start Word, your document appears in the Normal view.

1 To change to another view, move the mouse ⌖ over one of the options listed below (example: 📄) and then press the left button.

📄 Normal View

📄 Page Layout View

📄 Outline View

146

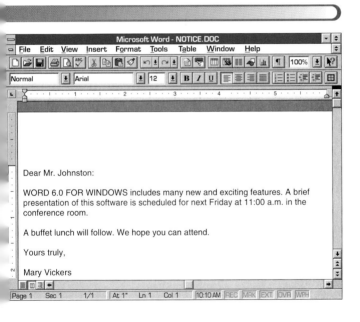

◆ Your document
appears in the new view
(example: **Page Layout**).

DISPLAY OR HIDE TOOLBARS

Word offers eight different toolbars that you can display or hide at any time.

DISPLAY OR HIDE TOOLBARS

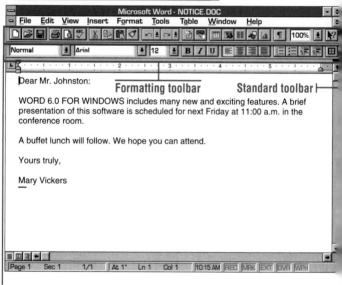

Formatting toolbar   Standard toolbar

◆ When you first start Word, the Standard and Formatting toolbars appear on your screen.

148

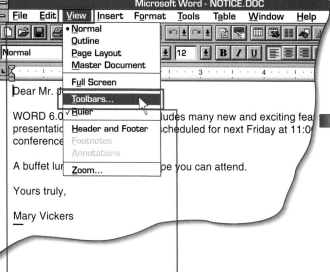

Microsoft Word - NOTICE.DOC

| File | Edit | View | Insert | Format | Tools | Table | Window | Help |

- • Normal
- Outline
- Page Layout
- Master Document

- Full Screen

- Toolbars...
- ✓ Ruler
- Header and Footer
- Footnotes
- Annotations
- Zoom...

Normal 12 B I U

Dear Mr.

WORD 6.0 ... ludes many new and exciting fea
presentatio ... scheduled for next Friday at 11:0
conference

A buffet lu ... pe you can attend.

Yours truly,

Mary Vickers

1 To display or hide a toolbar, move the mouse � over **View** and then press the left button.

2 Move the mouse � over **Toolbars** and then press the left button.

◆ The **Toolbars** dialog box appears.

Note: To continue, refer to the next page.

DISPLAY OR HIDE TOOLBARS

Each toolbar contains a series of buttons that let you quickly choose commands.

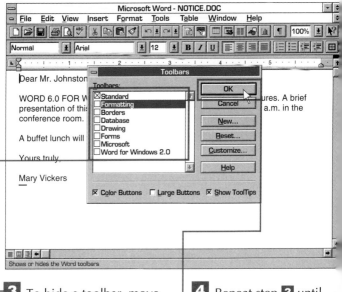

3 To hide a toolbar, move the mouse ⬚ over the toolbar name (example: **Formatting**) and then press the left button (⊠ changes to ☐).

◆ To display a toolbar, move the mouse ⬚ over the toolbar name and then press the left button (☐ changes to ⊠).

4 Repeat step **3** until you have selected all the toolbars you want to hide or display.

5 Move the mouse ⬚ over **OK** and then press the left button.

150

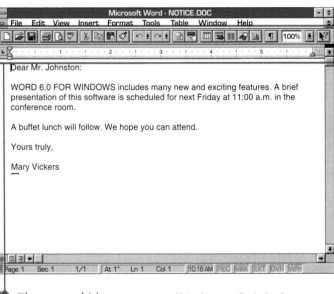

◆ The screen hides or displays the toolbar(s) you selected.

Note: A screen displaying fewer toolbars provides a larger and less cluttered working area.

DISPLAY OR HIDE TOOLBARS

You can quickly display or hide a toolbar by using the right button on your mouse.

QUICKLY DISPLAY OR HIDE A TOOLBAR

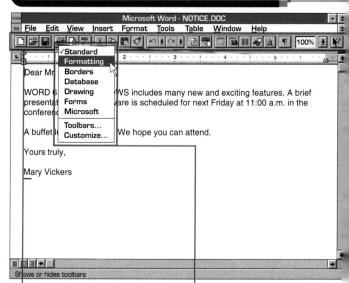

1 Move the mouse ▷ anywhere over a toolbar displayed on your screen and then press the **right** mouse button.

◆ A list of the available toolbars appears.

2 Move the mouse ▷ over the toolbar you want to display or hide and then press the left button.

Note: A √ beside a toolbar name tells you the toolbar is currently displayed on your screen.

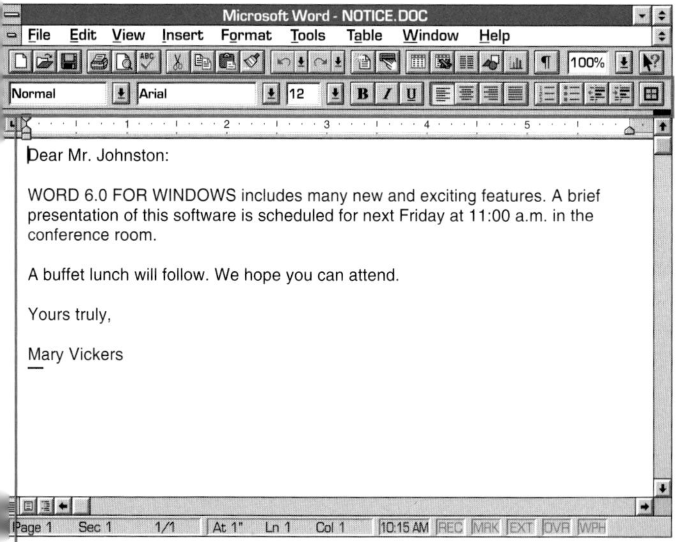

```
                    Microsoft Word - NOTICE.DOC
  File  Edit  View  Insert  Format  Tools  Table  Window  Help
```

Dear Mr. Johnston:

WORD 6.0 FOR WINDOWS includes many new and exciting features. A brief presentation of this software is scheduled for next Friday at 11:00 a.m. in the conference room.

A buffet lunch will follow. We hope you can attend.

Yours truly,

Mary Vickers

```
Page 1   Sec 1      1/1      At 1"   Ln 1   Col 1      10:15 AM  REC  MRK  EXT  OVR  WPH
```

◆ The screen displays
or hides the toolbar
you selected.

DISPLAY OR HIDE THE RULER

> The Ruler lets you indent paragraphs and change margin and tab settings. If you are not using the ruler, you can hide it to provide a larger and less cluttered working area.

DISPLAY OR HIDE THE RULER

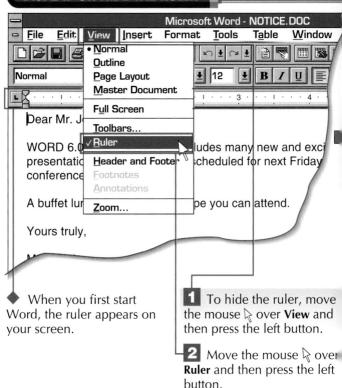

Microsoft Word - NOTICE.DOC

File   Edit   View   Insert   Format   Tools   Table   Window

- Normal
- Outline
- Page Layout
- Master Document
- Full Screen
- Toolbars...
- ✓ Ruler
- Header and Footer
- Footnotes
- Annotations
- Zoom...

Dear Mr. J

WORD 6.0 ...ludes many new and exci
presentatio ...scheduled for next Friday
conference

A buffet lu... pe you can attend.

Yours truly,

◆ When you first start Word, the ruler appears on your screen.

1 To hide the ruler, move the mouse ⟍ over **View** and then press the left button.

2 Move the mouse ⟍ over **Ruler** and then press the left button.

154

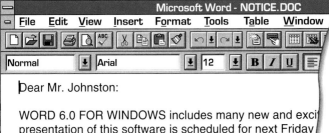

Microsoft Word - NOTICE.DOC

File Edit View Insert Format Tools Table Window

Normal   Arial   12   B I U

Dear Mr. Johnston:

WORD 6.0 FOR WINDOWS includes many new and excit
presentation of this software is scheduled for next Friday
conference room.

A buffet lunch will follow. We hope you can attend.

Yours truly,

Mary Vickers

◆ The **Ruler** disappears
from your screen.

To again display the ruler,
repeat steps **1** and **2**.

USING FULL SCREEN VIEW

USING FULL SCREEN VIEW

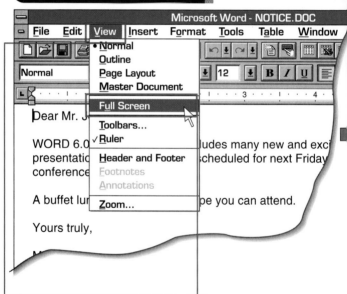

1 To use the Full Screen view, move the mouse ⤢ over **View** and then press the left button.

2 Move the mouse ⤢ over **Full Screen** and then press the left button.

156

You can use the Full Screen view to display more of your document. This will hide all screen elements such as the ruler, menu and toolbars to provide you with more working area.

Dear Mr. Johnston:

WORD 6.0 FOR WINDOWS includes many new and exciting features. A brief presentation of this software is scheduled for next Friday at 11:00 a.m. in the conference room.

A buffet lunch will follow. We hope you can attend.

Yours truly,

Mary Vickers

◆ Word uses the entire screen to display the text in your document.

3 To return to the previous view, move the mouse ⟍ over ▣ and then press the left button **or** press **Alt**, **V**, **U**.

BOLD, ITALICS AND UNDERLINE

bold | *italic* | underline

BOLD, ITALICIZE AND UNDERLINE TEXT

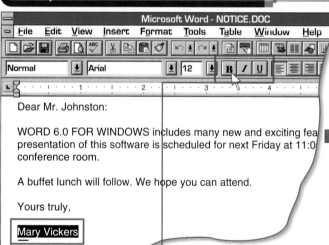

```
                        Microsoft Word - NOTICE.DOC
 File   Edit   View   Insert   Format   Tools   Table   Window   Help

 Normal      Arial              12      B  I  U

      1         2         3         4
```

Dear Mr. Johnston:

WORD 6.0 FOR WINDOWS includes many new and exciting fea
presentation of this software is scheduled for next Friday at 11:0
conference room.

A buffet lunch will follow. We hope you can attend.

Yours truly,

Mary Vickers

1 Select the text you want to change.

Note: To select text, refer to pages 28 to 31.

2 Move the mouse ⇩ over one of the following options and then press the left button.

B Bold text

I Italicize text

U Underline text

You can use the Bold, Italic and Underline features to emphasize important information. This will improve the overall appearance of your document.

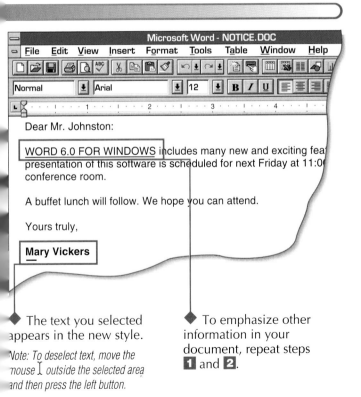

Microsoft Word - NOTICE.DOC

File   Edit   View   Insert   Format   Tools   Table   Window   Help

Normal   Arial   12   **B** *I* <u>U</u>

Dear Mr. Johnston:

<u>WORD 6.0 FOR WINDOWS</u> includes many new and exciting fea presentation of this software is scheduled for next Friday at 11:0 conference room.

A buffet lunch will follow. We hope you can attend.

Yours truly,

Mary Vickers

◆ The text you selected appears in the new style.

Note: To deselect text, move the mouse I outside the selected area and then press the left button.

◆ To emphasize other information in your document, repeat steps **1** and **2**.

CHANGE FONTS

CHANGE FONTS

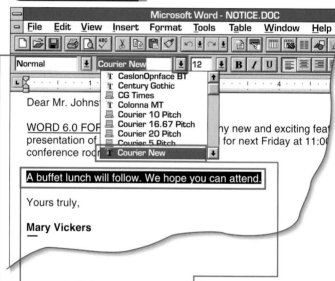

Microsoft Word - NOTICE.DOC

File   Edit   View   Insert   Format   Tools   Table   Window   Help

Normal   Courier New   12   B   I   U

T CaslonOpnface BT
T Century Gothic
CG Times
T Colonna MT
Courier 10 Pitch
Courier 16.67 Pitch
Courier 20 Pitch
Courier 5 Pitch
Courier New

Dear Mr. Johns

WORD 6.0 FOR   ny new and exciting feat
presentation of   for next Friday at 11:0(
conference roo

A buffet lunch will follow. We hope you can attend.

Yours truly,

Mary Vickers

1 Select the text you want to change to a new font.

Note: To select text, refer to pages 28 to 31.

2 To display a list of the available fonts, move the mouse ⌖ over ▼ beside the **Font** box and then press the left button.

3 Press ▼ or ▲ on your keyboard until you highlight the font you want to use (example: **Courier New**) and then press **Enter**.

160

You can change
the design of characters in
your document to emphasize
headings and make text
easier to read.

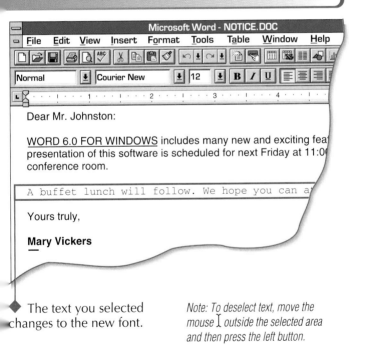

The text you selected
changes to the new font.

*Note: To deselect text, move the
mouse ⌶ outside the selected area
and then press the left button.*

CHANGE FONTS

You can increase or decrease the size of text in your document.

CHANGE FONT SIZE

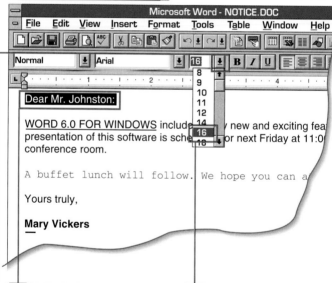

1 Select the text you want to change to a new font size.

Note: To select text, refer to pages 28 to 31.

2 To display a list of the available font sizes, move the mouse ⟍ over ⬇ beside the **Font Size** box and then press the left button.

3 Press ⬇ or ⬆ on your keyboard until you highlight the font size you want to use (example: **16**) and then press **Enter**.

162

6 point
12 point
14 point
18 point
24 point

Word measures the size of text in points. There are approximately 72 points per inch.

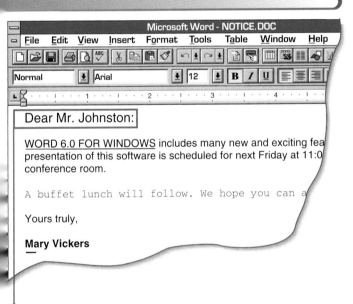

Microsoft Word - NOTICE.DOC

File   Edit   View   Insert   Format   Tools   Table   Window   Help

Normal | Arial | 12 | **B** *I* U

Dear Mr. Johnston:

WORD 6.0 FOR WINDOWS includes many new and exciting fea
presentation of this software is scheduled for next Friday at 11:0
conference room.

A buffet lunch will follow. We hope you can a

Yours truly,

Mary Vickers

◆ The text you selected changes to the new font size.

Note: To deselect text, move the mouse Ɪᵪ outside the selected area and then press the left button.

CHANGE FONTS

CHANGE FONTS

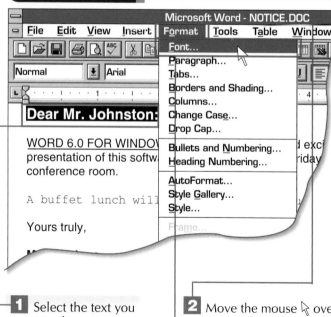

Microsoft Word - NOTICE.DOC

File   Edit   View   Insert   **Format**   Tools   Table   **Wi**ndow

Font...
Paragraph...
Tabs...
Borders and Shading...
Columns...
Change Case...
Drop Cap...

Bullets and Numbering...
Heading Numbering...

AutoFormat...
Style Gallery...
Style...

Frame...

Normal   Arial

Dear Mr. Johnston:

WORD 6.0 FOR WINDOW... d exci
presentation of this softw... riday
conference room.

A buffet lunch will

Yours truly,

1 Select the text you want to change.

Note: To select text, refer to pages 28 to 31.

2 Move the mouse ▷ over **Format** and then press the left button.

3 Move the mouse ▷ over **Font** and then press the left button.

164

You can change
the design and size
of characters in your
document at the same
time by using the
Font dialog box.

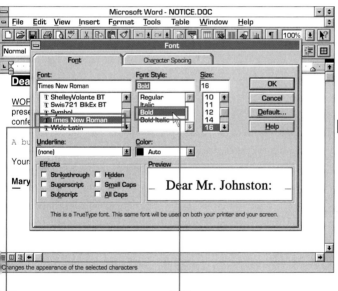

4 Move the mouse ⬚ over
the font you want to use
(example: **Times New Roman**)
and then press the left button.

*Note: To view all of the available font
options, use the scroll bar. To use the
scroll bar, refer to page 26.*

5 Move the mouse ⬚ over
the font style you want to use
(example: **Bold**) and then
press the left button.

Note: To continue, refer to the next page.

165

CHANGE FONTS

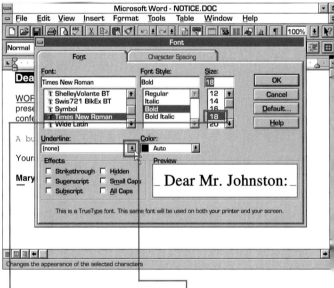

6 Move the mouse ⬚ over the font size you want to use (example: **18**) and then press the left button.

7 To select an underline style, move the mouse ⬚ over ⬚ in the **Underline:** box and then press the left button.

You can change the font of text to turn a dull, lifeless letter into an interesting, attractive document.

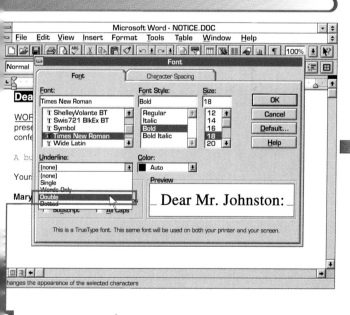

Move the mouse ⍰ over the underline style you want to use (example: **Double**) and then press the left button.

Note: To continue, refer to the next page.

167

The Font dialog box offers several effects that you can apply to text in your document.

CHANGE FONTS (Continued)

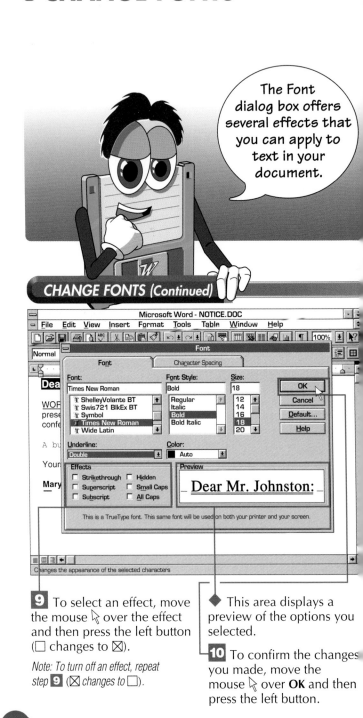

9 To select an effect, move the mouse ⤢ over the effect and then press the left button (☐ changes to ☒).

Note: To turn off an effect, repeat step **9** *(☒ changes to ☐).*

◆ This area displays a preview of the options you selected.

10 To confirm the changes you made, move the mouse ⤢ over **OK** and then press the left button.

~~Strikethrough~~

Text^{Superscript}

Text_{Subscript}

SMALL CAPS

ALL CAPS

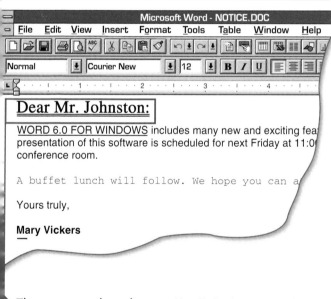

Microsoft Word - NOTICE.DOC

File   Edit   View   Insert   Format   Tools   Table   Window   Help

Normal ⬦ Courier New ⬦ 12 ⬦ **B** *I* U

Dear Mr. Johnston:

WORD 6.0 FOR WINDOWS includes many new and exciting fea
presentation of this software is scheduled for next Friday at 11:0
conference room.

A buffet lunch will follow. We hope you can a

Yours truly,

Mary Vickers

► The text you selected
isplays the font changes.

Note: To deselect text, move the mouse I outside the selected area and then press the left button.

INSERT A SYMBOL

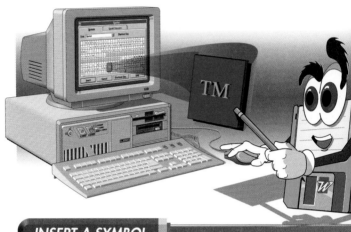

INSERT A SYMBOL

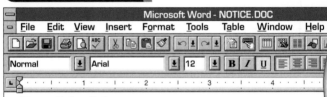

Dear Mr. Johnston:

WORD 6.0 FOR WINDOWS includes many new and exciting fea
presentation of this software is scheduled for next Friday at 11:0(
conference room.

A buffet lunch will follow. We hope you can a

Yours truly,

Mary Vickers

1 Position the insertion
point where you want a
symbol to appear in your
document.

170

Word lets you insert symbols into your document that are not displayed on your keyboard.

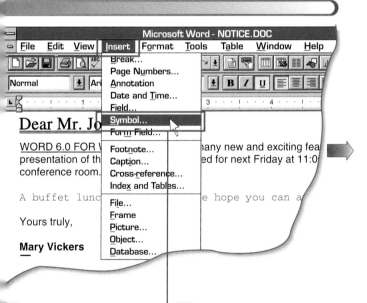

Microsoft Word - NOTICE.DOC

File   Edit   View   **Insert**   Format   Tools   Table   Window   Help

Normal

Break...
Page Numbers...
Annotation
Date and Time...
Field...
Symbol...
Form Field...
Footnote...
Caption...
Cross-reference...
Index and Tables...
File...
Frame
Picture...
Object...
Database...

Dear Mr. J

WORD 6.0 FOR ___ many new and exciting fea
presentation of th ___ ed for next Friday at 11:0
conference room.

A buffet lunc ___ e hope you can a

Yours truly,

Mary Vickers

2 Move the mouse ⌖ over **Insert** and then press the left button.

3 Move the mouse ⌖ over **Symbol** and then press the left button.

Note: To continue, refer to the next page.

171

INSERT A SYMBOL

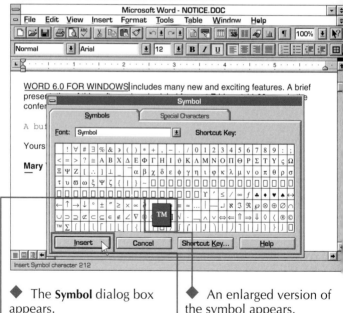

◆ The **Symbol** dialog box appears.

4 Move the mouse ⌖ over the symbol you want to insert (example: **TM**) and then press the left button.

◆ An enlarged version of the symbol appears.

5 To insert the symbol into your document, move the mouse ⌖ over **Insert** and then press the left button.

172

Word offers a wide selection of symbols. For example, you can insert the ™, ®, ♣, Σ, or © symbol into your document.

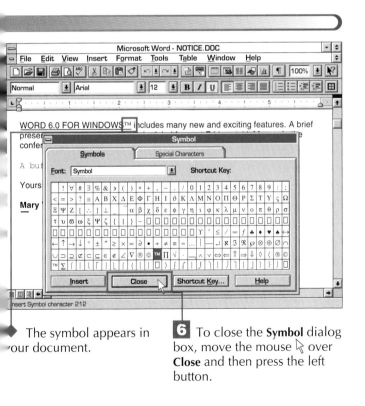

◆ The symbol appears in your document.

6 To close the **Symbol** dialog box, move the mouse ⤢ over **Close** and then press the left button.

CHANGE PARAGRAPH ALIGNMENT

You can enhance the appearance of your document by aligning text in different ways. Word offers four alignment options.

CHANGE PARAGRAPH ALIGNMENT

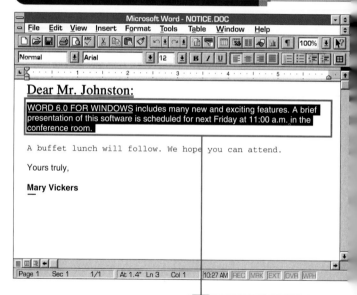

Word automatically left aligns any text you type in your document.

1 Select the paragraph(s) you want to change.

Note: To select text, refer to pages 28 to 31.

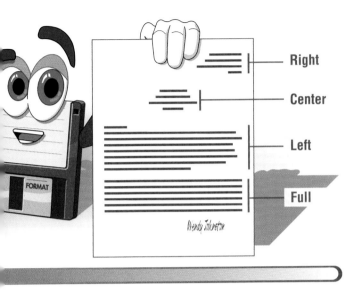

Right

Center

Left

Full

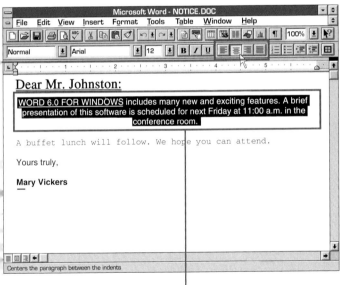

Centers the paragraph between the indents

2 Move the mouse ⇦ over one of the following options and then press the left button.

◆ Word changes the alignment of the paragraph(s) you selected.

▤ Left align paragraph

▤ Center paragraph

▤ Right align paragraph

▤ Fully align paragraph

175

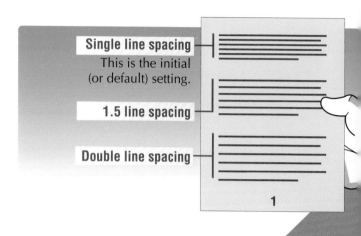

Single line spacing
This is the initial (or default) setting.

1.5 line spacing

Double line spacing

1

CHANGE LINE SPACING

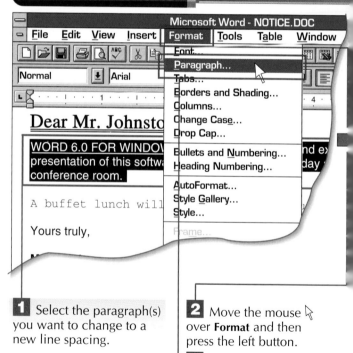

1 Select the paragraph(s) you want to change to a new line spacing.

Note: To select text, refer to pages 28 to 31.

2 Move the mouse ⌖ over **Format** and then press the left button.

3 Move the mouse ⌖ over **Paragraph** and then press the left button.

When you type text, Word automatically single spaces the text. You can change the line spacing at any time.

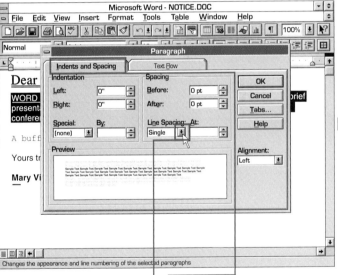

◆ The **Paragraph** dialog box appears.

4 Move the mouse ↳ over the **Indents and Spacing** tab and then press the left button.

5 Move the mouse ↳ over ▣ in the **Line Spacing:** box and then press the left button.

Note: To continue, refer to the next page.

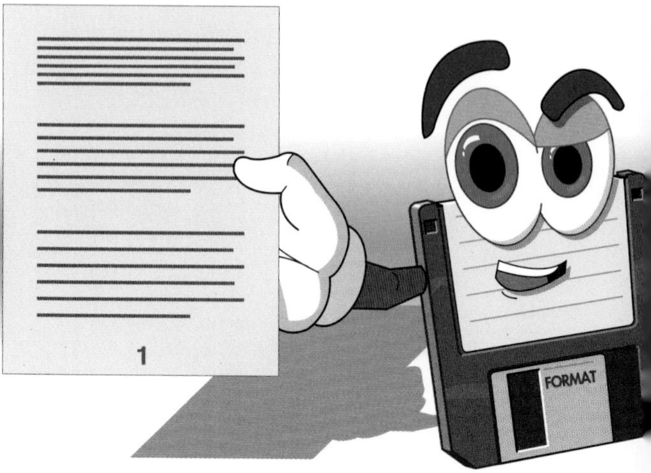

CHANGE LINE SPACING (Continued)

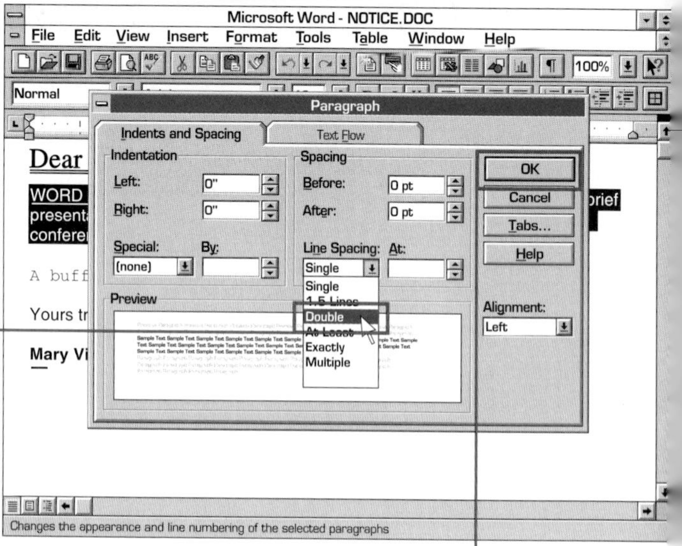

◆ A list of the available line spacing options appears.

6 Move the mouse over the line spacing you want to use (example: **Double**) and then press the left button.

7 Move the mouse over **OK** and then press the left button.

You can make your document easier to read by changing the line spacing.

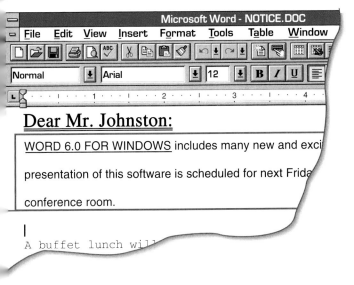

Word changes the line spacing of the paragraph(s) you selected.

Note: To deselect text, move the mouse I outside the selected area and then press the left button.

ADD A TAB STOP

> You can use tabs to line up columns of information in your document. Word offers four types of tabs.

ADD A TAB STOP

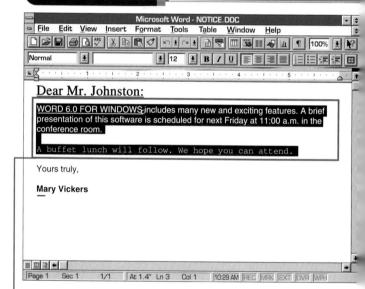

1 Select the paragraph(s) you want to contain the new tab stops.

Note: To select text, refer to pages 28 to 31.

◆ To add tab stops to text you are about to type, position the insertion point where you want to begin typing the text.

Left tab

Right tab

Center tab

123.45 (Decimal tab)

Tab stop position

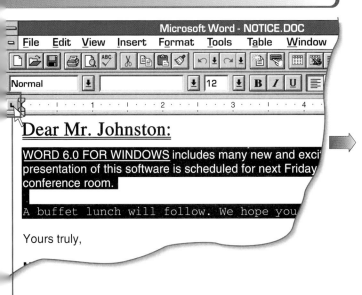

Microsoft Word - NOTICE.DOC

File   Edit   View   Insert   Format   Tools   Table   Window

Normal   ⬇   ⬇ 12   ⬇   **B** *I* U

Dear Mr. Johnston:

WORD 6.0 FOR WINDOWS includes many new and exci
presentation of this software is scheduled for next Friday
conference room.

A buffet lunch will follow. We hope you

Yours truly,

2 Move the mouse ⬚ over
this box and then press the left
button. Repeat this step until
the type of tab you want to add
appears (example: ⬛).

*Note: If the ruler is not displayed on your
screen, refer to page 154.*

⬛	**Left tab**
⬛	**Center tab**
⬛	**Right tab**
⬛	**Decimal tab**

*Note: To continue, refer to
the next page.*

ADD A TAB STOP

Make sure you use tabs rather than spaces to line up columns of text. This will ensure your document prints correctly.

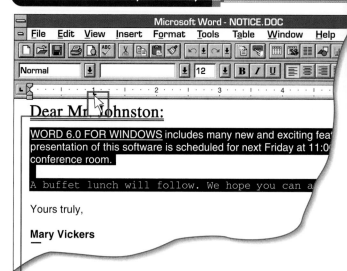

3 Move the mouse ⬚ over the position on the ruler where you want to add the tab stop and then press the left button.

Note: Make sure you position the mouse ⬚ over the lower half of the ruler.

◆ The new tab stop appears on the ruler.

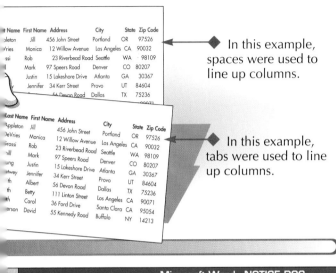

◆ In this example, spaces were used to line up columns.

◆ In this example, tabs were used to line up columns.

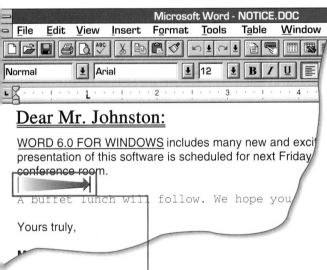

Microsoft Word - NOTICE.DOC

File   Edit   View   Insert   Format   Tools   Table   Window

Normal   Arial   12   B I U

Dear Mr. Johnston:

WORD 6.0 FOR WINDOWS includes many new and exci
presentation of this software is scheduled for next Friday
conference room.

A buffet lunch will follow. We hope you

Yours truly,

fter you have set tabs,
ou can use them to
uickly move the insertion
oint across your screen.

Using Tabs

1 Position the insertion point at the beginning of the line you want to move across.

2 Press Tab . The insertion point and any text that follows moves to the first tab stop.

MOVE A TAB STOP

You can easily move a tab stop to a different location on the ruler.

MOVE A TAB STOP

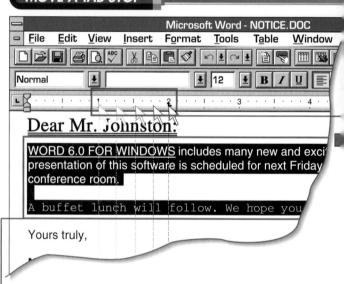

1 Select the paragraph(s) containing the tab stop you want to move.

2 Move the mouse ⌖ over the tab stop and then press and hold down the left button as you drag the tab stop to a new position.

◆ A dotted line indicates the new tab stop position.

184

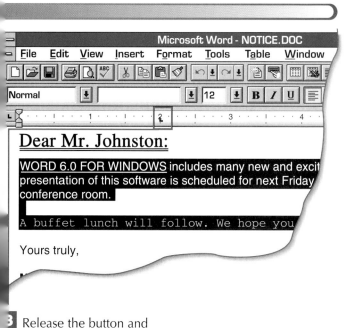

3 Release the button and
the tab stop moves to the
new position.

REMOVE A TAB STOP

Word lets you remove a tab stop from the ruler.

Dear Mr. Johnston:

WORD 6.0 FOR WINDOWS includes many new and exciting features. A brief presentation of this software is scheduled for next Friday at 11:00 a.m. in the conference room.

REMOVE A TAB STOP

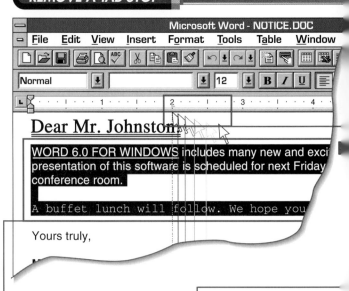

1 Select the paragraph(s) containing the tab stop you want to remove.

2 Move the mouse ⌖ over the tab stop and then press and hold down the left button as you drag the tab stop downward off the ruler.

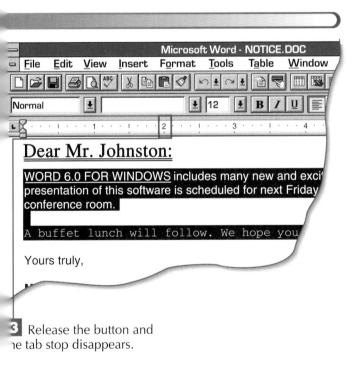

Microsoft Word - NOTICE.DOC

File   Edit   View   Insert   Format   Tools   Table   Window

Normal   12   **B** *I* U

Dear Mr. Johnston:

WORD 6.0 FOR WINDOWS includes many new and exci
presentation of this software is scheduled for next Friday
conference room.

A buffet lunch will follow. We hope you

Yours truly,

3 Release the button and
the tab stop disappears.

INDENT PARAGRAPHS

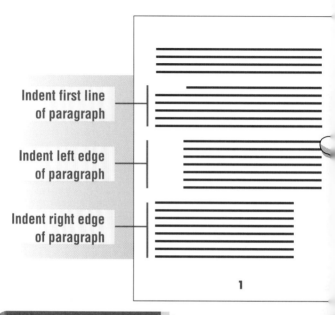

Indent first line
of paragraph

Indent left edge
of paragraph

Indent right edge
of paragraph

1

INDENT PARAGRAPHS

You can move these symbols on the ruler to indent
paragraphs in your document.

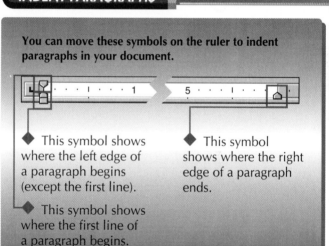

◆ This symbol shows
where the left edge of
a paragraph begins
(except the first line).

◆ This symbol shows
where the first line of
a paragraph begins.

◆ This symbol
shows where the right
edge of a paragraph
ends.

You can use the Indent feature to emphasize paragraphs in your document. Word offers several indent options.

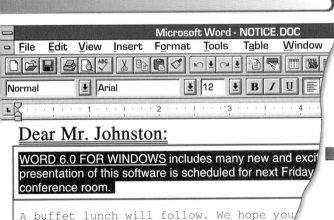

1 Select the paragraph(s) you want to indent.

Note: To select text, refer to pages 28 to 31.

Note: To continue, refer to the next page.

INDENT PARAGRAPHS

To indent paragraphs in your document, make sure the ruler is displayed on your screen.

Note: To display the ruler, refer to page 154.

INDENT PARAGRAPHS (Continued)

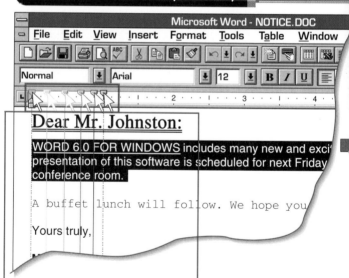

2 Move the mouse ⬚ over the symbol you want to move (example: ▽) and then press and hold down the left button.

3 Still holding down the button, move the mouse ⬚ where you want to position the symbol.

190

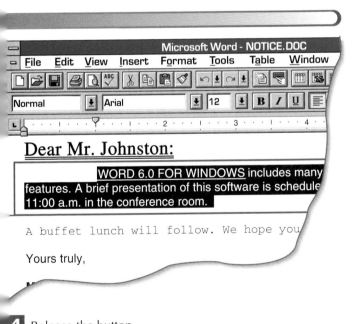

4 Release the button and Word indents the paragraph(s) you selected.

CREATE NUMBERED AND BULLETED LISTS

You can emphasize text in a list by beginning each item with a bullet or number.

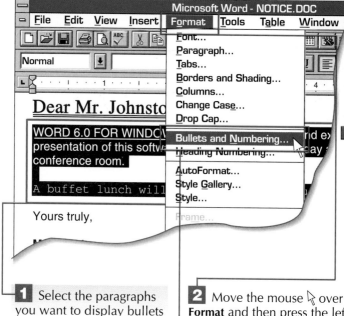

1 Select the paragraphs you want to display bullets or numbers.

Note: To select text, refer to pages 28 to 31.

2 Move the mouse ⟍ over **Format** and then press the left button.

3 Move the mouse ⟍ over **Bullets and Numbering** and then press the left button.

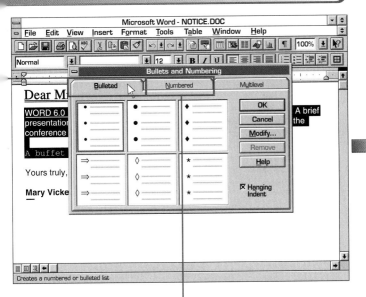

◆ The **Bullets and Numbering** dialog box appears.

4 To create a bulleted list, move the mouse ⌖ over the **Bulleted** tab and then press the left button.

◆ To create a numbered list, move the mouse ⌖ over the **Numbered** tab and then press the left button.

Note: To continue, refer to the next page.

CREATE NUMBERED AND BULLETED LISTS

A bulleted list is useful for items in no particular order, like a list of goals. A numbered list is useful for items in a specific order, like a recipe.

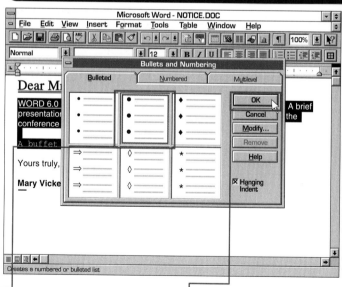

5 Move the mouse ⌖ over the style you want to use and then press the left button.

6 Move the mouse ⌖ over **OK** and then press the left button.

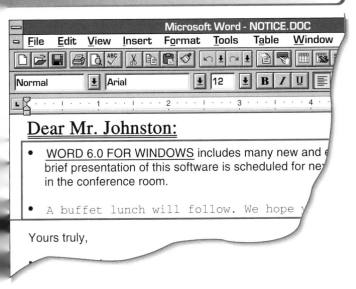

◆ The bullets or numbers appear in your document.

Note: To deselect text, move the mouse I outside the selected area and then press the left button.

INSERT A PAGE BREAK

If you want to start a new page at a specific place in your document, you can insert a page break.

INSERT A PAGE BREAK

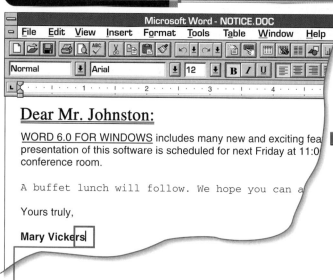

1 Position the insertion point where you want to start a new page.

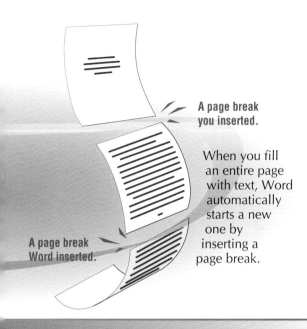

A page break you inserted.

When you fill an entire page with text, Word automatically starts a new one by inserting a page break.

A page break Word inserted.

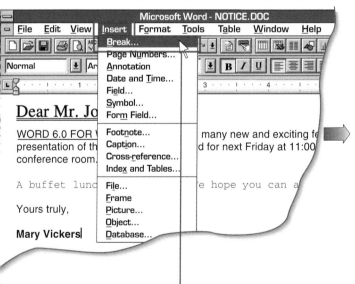

Microsoft Word - NOTICE.DOC

File   Edit   View   Insert   Format   Tools   Table   Window   Help

Break...
Page Numbers...
Annotation
Date and Time...
Field...
Symbol...
Form Field...

Normal

Dear Mr. Jo

WORD 6.0 FOR   Footnote...   many new and exciting fe
presentation of th   Caption...   d for next Friday at 11:00
conference room.   Cross-reference...
                   Index and Tables...

A buffet lunc   File...   e hope you can a
                  Frame
Yours truly,   Picture...
                  Object...
Mary Vickers   Database...

2 Move the mouse ⃗ over **Insert** and then press the left button.

3 Move the mouse ⃗ over **Break** and then press the left button.

Note: To continue, refer to the next page.

197

INSERT A PAGE BREAK

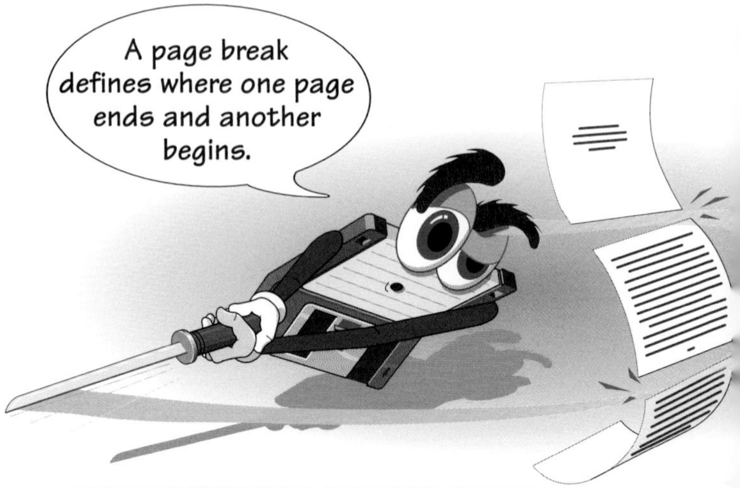

INSERT A PAGE BREAK (Continued)

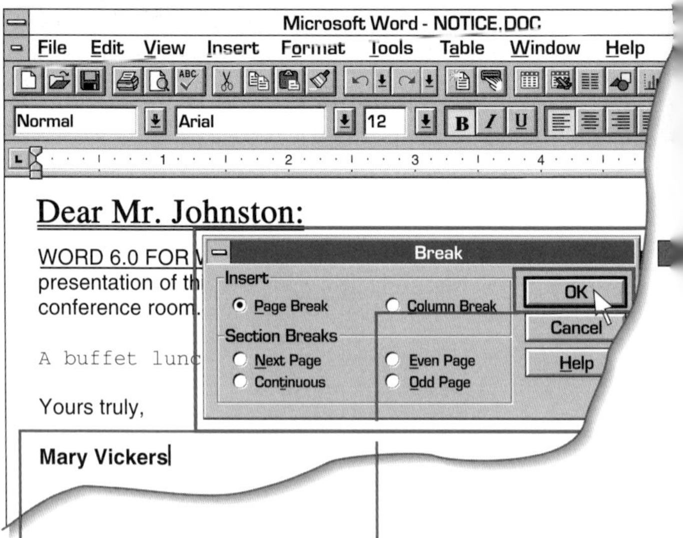

◆ The **Break** dialog box appears.

4 Move the mouse over **OK** and then press the left button.

To quickly insert a page break:

1 Position the insertion point where you want to start a new page.

2 Press `Ctrl` + `Enter`.

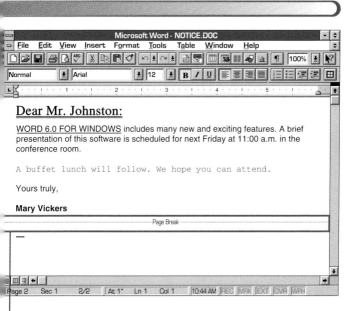

◆ If your document is in the Normal view, a dotted line with the words **Page Break** appears across your screen. This line defines where one page ends and another begins.

*Note: The **Page Break** line will not appear when you print your document.*

DELETE A PAGE BREAK

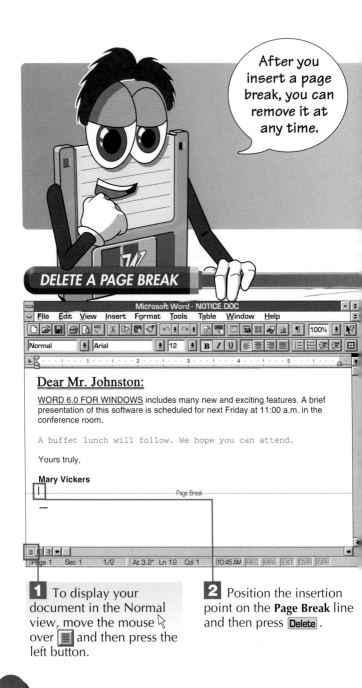

After you insert a page break, you can remove it at any time.

DELETE A PAGE BREAK

1 To display your document in the Normal view, move the mouse ↖ over ▤ and then press the left button.

2 Position the insertion point on the **Page Break** line and then press Delete.

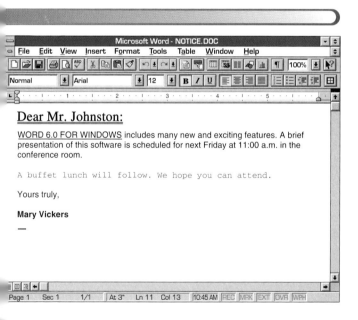

◆ The **Page Break** line disappears.

CHANGE MARGINS

CHANGE MARGINS

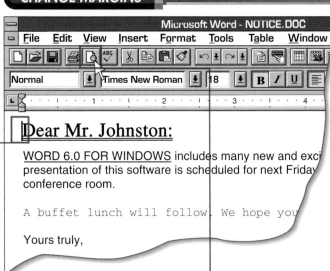

1 To change the margins for your entire document, position the insertion point anywhere in the document.

2 Move the mouse ⌖ over 🔍 and then press the left button.

202

> A margin is the amount of space between the text and the edges of your paper.

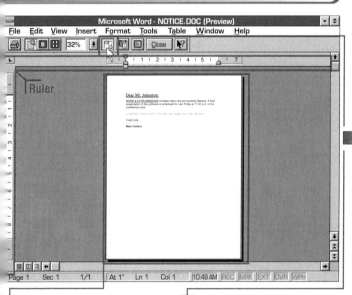

◆ The page you were working on appears in the Print Preview window.

Note: For more information on using Print Preview, refer to pages 132 to 139.

3 If the ruler is not displayed, move the mouse ⟍ over 🖼 and then press the left button.

Note: To continue, refer to the next page.

CHANGE MARGINS

When you create a document, the top and bottom margins are set at 1 inch. The left and right margins are set at 1.25 inches. You can easily change these settings.

CHANGE MARGINS (Continued)

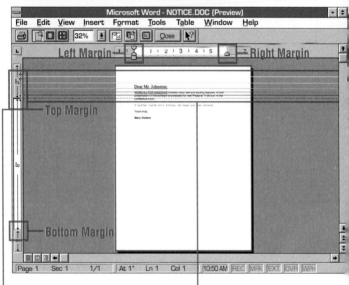

4 Move the mouse ⅓ over the margin boundary you want to move and ⅓ changes to ↕ or ↔.

5 To display the page measurements as you drag the margin boundary, press and hold down `Alt`.

6 Still holding down `Alt`, press and hold down the left button as you drag the margin boundary to a new location. A dotted line shows the location of the new margin.

TIP

If you only want to change the left and right margins for a part of your document, it is much easier to change the indentation.

Note: To indent paragraphs, refer to page 188.

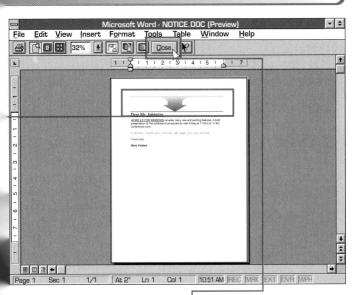

7 Release the button and then Alt to display the margin changes.

8 Repeat steps **4** to **7** for each margin you want to change.

9 To close Print Preview and return to your document, move the mouse ⬚ over **Close** and then press the left button.

Note: The top and bottom margins are not visible on your screen when in the Normal view.

205

ADD HEADERS OR FOOTERS

Headers display information at the top of each page. Footers display information at the bottom of each page. They may include the title of your document, the date or your company name.

ADD HEADERS OR FOOTERS

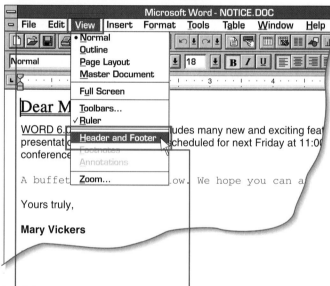

1 To add a header or footer to every page in your document, move the mouse over **View** and then press the left button.

2 Move the mouse over **Header and Footer** and then press the left button.

Header ◆

GLOBAL REPORT

Seventy-five percent of the World's people live in the Third World. These nations supply the developed nations with a multitude of raw materials and natural resources, and also buy many of our exports, (40% of U.S. exports are bought by the Third World). Clearly the lives of the people in the developed and underdeveloped worlds are unavoidably interrelated. It is for this reason that it is important for the rich nations to study the problems in other countries and help them to overcome them.

One major problem in most underdeveloped countries (UDC), is that since the Colonial period, exploitation of their arable land has rapidly increased. Companies from the developed countries (DC) are blamed for abusing the land, but the farmers and locals are often guilty as well. 75% of the energy supplied in the UDC's is produced by wood burning. To get this wood they must tear down trees, and eventually whole forests disappear. The land then no longer has anything holding it together. This results in soil erosion and loss water retaining abilities.

Development in the Western sense is to industrialize your economy. It is essential for the Third World to develop their production techniques, especially in agriculture, in order to compete effectively on the World Markets. This kind of development, however, requires not only costly machinery, but expensive fossil fuels for operation. For countries already billions in debt this is obviously not economically possible.

CHAPTER 1 ◆ **Footer**

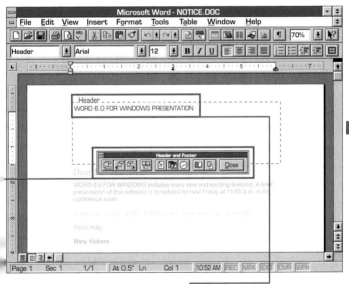

◆ The text in your document appears dimmed.

◆ The **Header and Footer** toolbar appears.

3 To create a header, type the header text. You can format the header text as you would any text in your document.

Note: To continue, refer to the next page.

ADD HEADERS OR FOOTERS

Headers and footers will not appear on your screen if you are in the Normal view.

CHAPTER 1

ADD HEADERS OR FOOTERS (Continued)

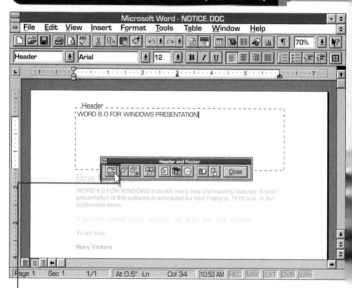

4 To create a footer, move the mouse ⌖ over 🖫 and then press the left button.

Note: You can return to the header area at any time by repeating step **4**.

208

TIP

To view headers or footers, move the mouse over and then press the left button.

Note: For more information on Print Preview, refer to pages 132 to 139.

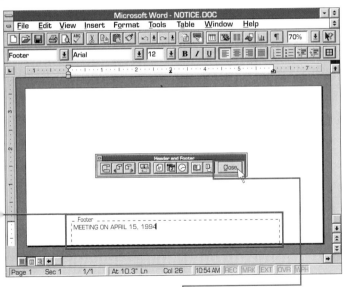

◆ The **Footer** area appears.

5 Type the footer text. You can format the footer text as you would any text in your document.

6 To return to your document, move the mouse over **Close** and then press the left button.

ADD PAGE NUMBERS

You can have Word automatically number the pages in your document.

ADD PAGE NUMBERS

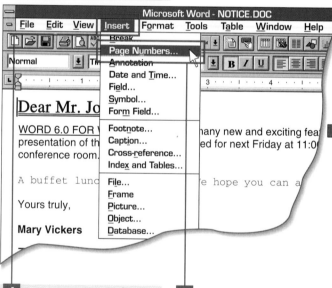

1 Move the mouse ⬧ over **Insert** and then press the left button.

2 Move the mouse ⬧ over **Page Numbers** and then press the left button.

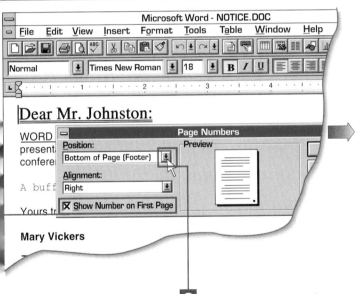

◆ The **Page Numbers** dialog box appears.

◆ To hide the page number on the first page of your document, move the mouse ⟍ over **Show Number on First Page** and then press the left button (☒ changes to ☐).

3 To select a position for the page numbers, move the mouse ⟍ over ⬇ in the **Position:** box and then press the left button.

Note: To continue, refer to the next page.

ADD PAGE NUMBERS

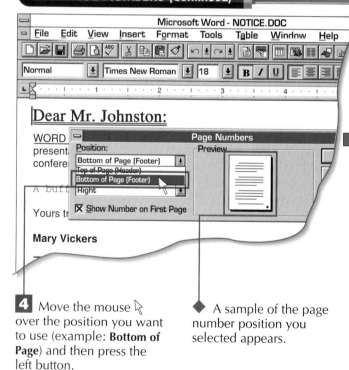

Page numbers will not appear on your screen if you are in the Normal view.

ADD PAGE NUMBERS (Continued)

Microsoft Word - NOTICE.DOC

File Edit View Insert Format Tools Table Window Help

Normal   Times New Roman   18   B I U

Dear Mr. Johnston:

WORD

present

confere

Page Numbers

Position:

Bottom of Page (Footer)

Top of Page (Header)

Bottom of Page (Footer)

Right

Preview

A buff

Yours tr

☒ Show Number on First Page

Mary Vickers

4 Move the mouse over the position you want to use (example: **Bottom of Page**) and then press the left button.

◆ A sample of the page number position you selected appears.

To view page numbers, move the mouse ⬚ over 🔍 and then press the left button.

Note: For more information on Print Preview, refer to pages 132 to 139.

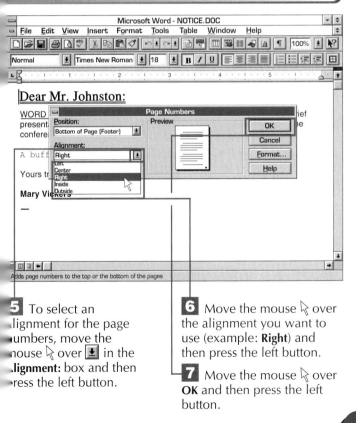

5 To select an alignment for the page numbers, move the mouse ⬚ over ⬚ in the **Alignment:** box and then press the left button.

6 Move the mouse ⬚ over the alignment you want to use (example: **Right**) and then press the left button.

7 Move the mouse ⬚ over **OK** and then press the left button.

CENTER A PAGE

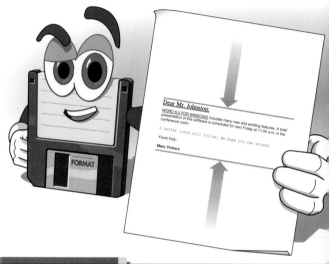

CENTER A PAGE

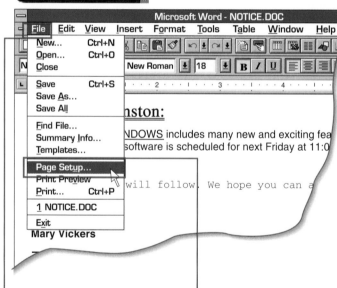

1 Move the mouse ⌖ over **File** and then press the left button.

2 Move the mouse ⌖ over **Page Setup** and then press the left button.

You can vertically center text on a page. This is useful when creating title pages or short memos.

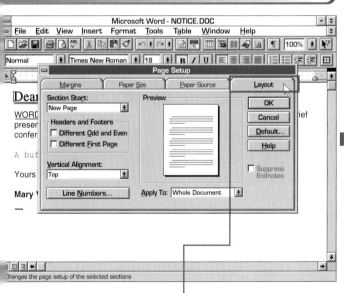

▶ The **Page Setup** dialog box appears.

3 Move the mouse ▷ over the **Layout** tab and then press the left button.

Note: To continue, refer to the next page.

215

CENTER A PAGE

Text will not appear centered on your screen if you are in the Normal view.

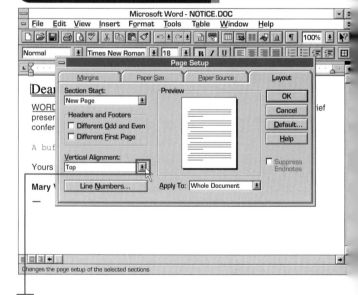

4 Move the mouse ☐ over ☐ in the **Vertical Alignment**: box and then press the left button.

216

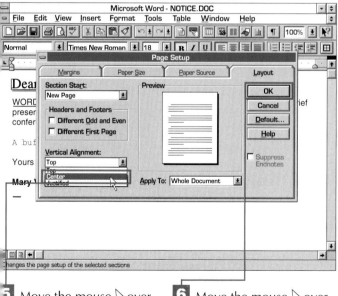

TIP

To view the text centered on a page, move the mouse ▷ over 🔍 and then press the left button.

Note: For more information on Print Preview, refer to pages 132 to 139.

Microsoft Word - NOTICE.DOC

File   Edit   View   Insert   Format   Tools   Table   Window   Help

Normal   Times New Roman   18   B *I* U

Page Setup

| Margins | Paper Size | Paper Source | Layout |

Section Start:
New Page

Headers and Footers
☐ Different Odd and Even
☐ Different First Page

Vertical Alignment:
Top
~~Top~~
Center
Justified

Preview

OK
Cancel
Default...
Help

☐ Suppress Endnotes

Apply To: Whole Document

Dea

WORD   ief
preser
confer

A buf

Yours

Mary

Changes the page setup of the selected sections

5 Move the mouse ▷ over **enter** and then press the left button.

6 Move the mouse ▷ over **OK** and then press the left button.

217

CREATE A TABLE

CREATE A TABLE

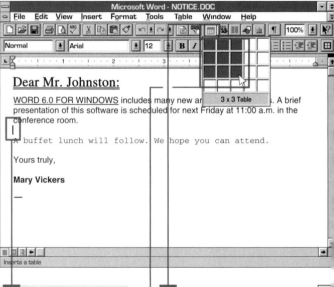

1 To create a table, position the insertion point where you want the table to appear in your document.

2 Move the mouse ⌖ over 🔳

3 Press and hold down the left button as you move the mouse ⌖ over the number of rows and columns you want in your table (example: **3 x 3**).

218

You can create a table to neatly organize your information. A table consists of columns, rows and cells.

◆ A **column** is a vertical line of boxes.

◆ A **row** is a horizontal line of boxes.

◆ A **cell** is the area where a row and column intersect.

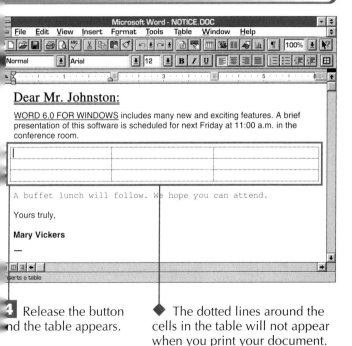

4 Release the button and the table appears.

◆ The dotted lines around the cells in the table will not appear when you print your document. To print table lines, you must add borders. For more information, refer to page 234.

TYPE TEXT IN A TABLE

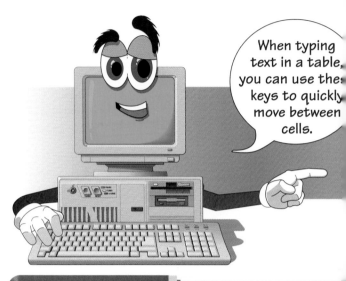

When typing text in a table, you can use these keys to quickly move between cells.

TYPE TEXT IN A TABLE

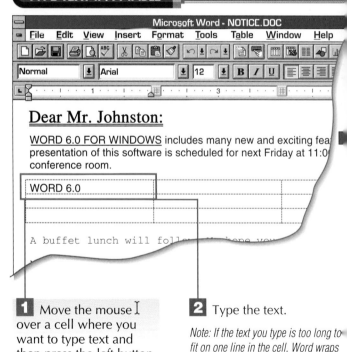

1 Move the mouse I over a cell where you want to type text and then press the left button.

2 Type the text.

Note: If the text you type is too long to fit on one line in the cell, Word wraps the text to the next line. To keep the text on the same line, refer to page 230 to change the column width.

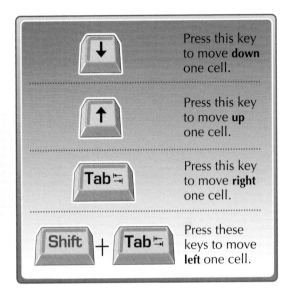

Press this key to move **down** one cell.

Press this key to move **up** one cell.

Press this key to move **right** one cell.

Press these keys to move **left** one cell.

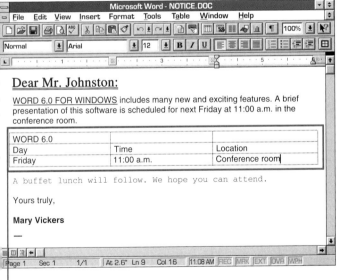

Microsoft Word - NOTICE.DOC

File Edit View Insert Format Tools Table Window Help

Normal   Arial   12   B I U

Dear Mr. Johnston:

WORD 6.0 FOR WINDOWS includes many new and exciting features. A brief presentation of this software is scheduled for next Friday at 11:00 a.m. in the conference room.

WORD 6.0		
Day	Time	Location
Friday	11:00 a.m.	Conference room

A buffet lunch will follow. We hope you can attend.

Yours truly,

Mary Vickers

Page 1   Sec 1   1/1   At 2.6" Ln 9   Col 16   11:08 AM   REC MRK EXT OVR WPH

3 Repeat steps **1** and **2** until you have typed all the text.

◆ Pressing **Enter** after typing text in a cell will begin a new line and increase the row height. If you accidentally press **Enter**, immediately press **←Backspace** to cancel the action.

ADD A ROW

You can add a row to your table if you want to insert new information.

ADD A ROW

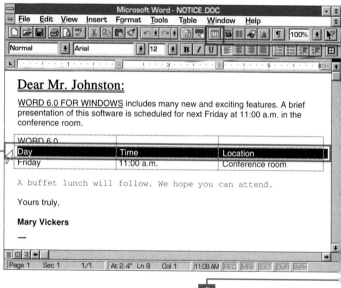

Word adds a row above the row you select.

1 To select a row, move the mouse I to the left edge of the row (I changes to ⤢) and then press the left button.

2 Move the mouse ⬚ over 🔳 and then press the left button.

222

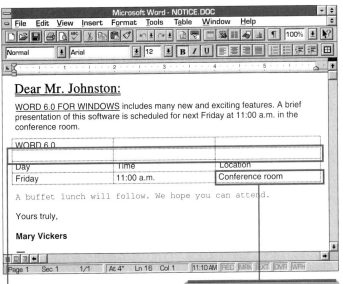

◆ The new row appears.

Note: To deselect a row, move the mouse ⅃ outside the table and then press the left button.

To add a row to the bottom of your table:

1 Position the insertion point in the bottom right cell of your table.

2 Press **Tab** and the new row appears.

ADD A COLUMN

You can add a column to your table at any time. The existing columns shift to make room for the new column.

ADD A COLUMN

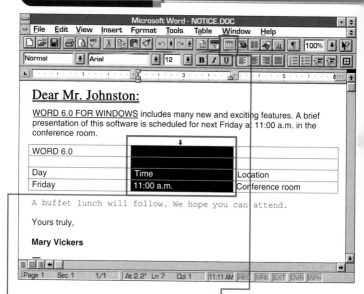

Word adds a column to the left of the column you select.

1 To select a column, move the mouse I to the top edge of the column (I changes to ↓) and then press the left button.

2 Move the mouse ↕ over [icon] and then press the left button.

224

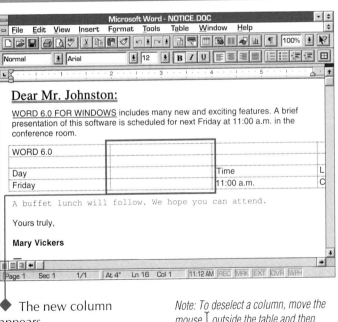

Microsoft Word - NOTICE.DOC

File Edit View Insert Format Tools Table Window Help

Normal   Arial   12   **B** *I* U

Dear Mr. Johnston:

WORD 6.0 FOR WINDOWS includes many new and exciting features. A brief presentation of this software is scheduled for next Friday at 11:00 a.m. in the conference room.

WORD 6.0			
Day		Time	L
Friday		11:00 a.m.	C

A buffet lunch will follow. We hope you can attend.

Yours truly,

Mary Vickers

Page 1   Sec 1   1/1   At 4"   Ln 16   Col 1   11:12 AM

◆ The new column appears.

Note: To deselect a column, move the mouse I outside the table and then press the left button.

DELETE A ROW

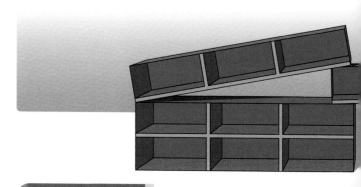

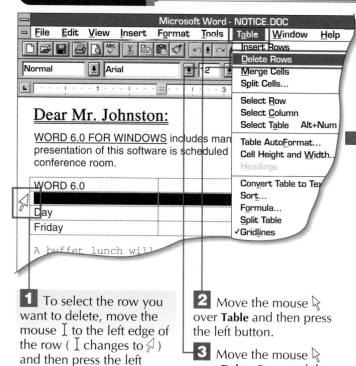

1 To select the row you want to delete, move the mouse I to the left edge of the row (I changes to ⇗) and then press the left button.

2 Move the mouse ⇗ over **Table** and then press the left button.

3 Move the mouse ⇗ over **Delete Rows** and then press the left button.

226

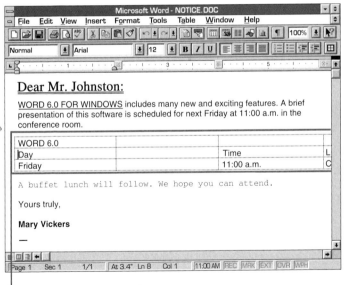

◆ The row disappears from your table.

DELETE A COLUMN

You can easily delete a column from your table. The remaining columns move to fill the empty space.

DELETE A COLUMN

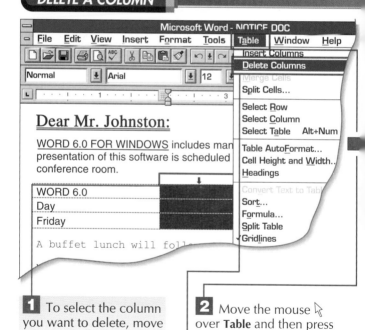

1 To select the column you want to delete, move the mouse I to the top edge of the column (I changes to ↓) and then press the left button.

2 Move the mouse ↕ over **Table** and then press the left button.

3 Move the mouse ↕ over **Delete Columns** and then press the left button.

228

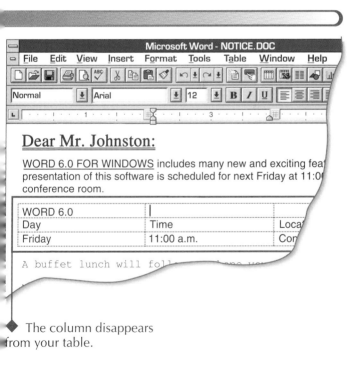

Microsoft Word - NOTICE.DOC

File   Edit   View   Insert   Format   Tools   Table   Window   Help

Normal   Arial   12   **B** *I* <u>U</u>

Dear Mr. Johnston:

<u>WORD 6.0 FOR WINDOWS</u> includes many new and exciting fea
presentation of this software is scheduled for next Friday at 11:0
conference room.

WORD 6.0		
Day	Time	Loca
Friday	11:00 a.m.	Con

A buffet lunch will fol

◆ The column disappears
from your table.

CHANGE COLUMN WIDTH

You can adjust the columns in your table to make them wider or narrower.

CHANGE COLUMN WIDTH

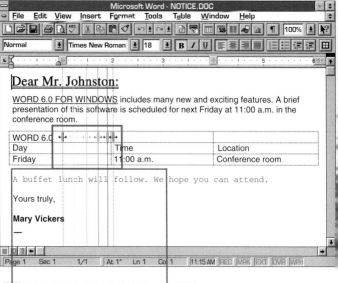

1 Move the mouse I over the right edge of the column you want to change (I changes to ⊹).

2 Press and hold down the left button as you drag the edge of the column to a new position.

◆ The dotted line indicates the new position.

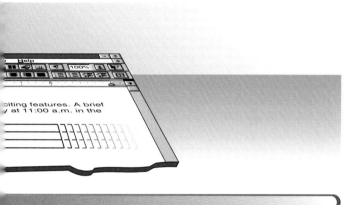

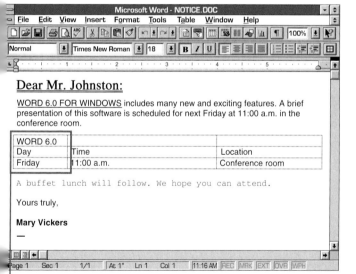

3 Release the button
nd the new column
idth appears.

Note: The width of the entire table remains the same.

CHANGE COLUMN WIDTH

You can have Word adjust a column width to fit the longest item in the column.

CHANGE COLUMN WIDTH AUTOMATICALLY

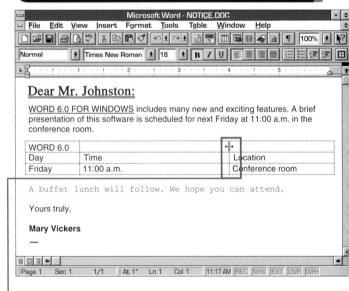

1 Move the mouse I over the right edge of the column you want to change (I changes to +‖+).

2 Quickly press the left button twice.

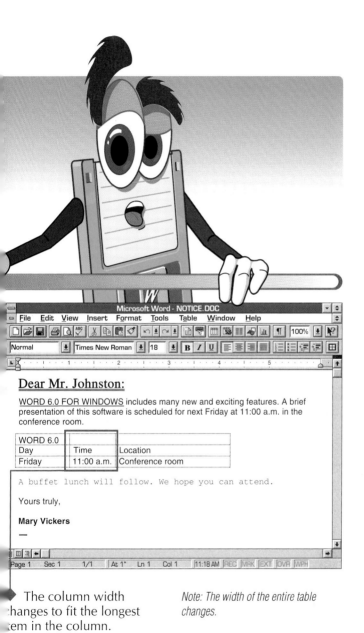

The column width changes to fit the longest item in the column.

Note: The width of the entire table changes.

FORMAT A TABLE

FORMAT A TABLE

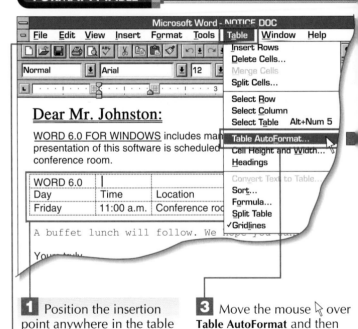

1 Position the insertion point anywhere in the table you want to format.

2 Move the mouse ⓀⓈ over **Table** and then press the left button.

3 Move the mouse ⓀⓈ over **Table AutoFormat** and then press the left button.

234

Word provides a selection of designs that you can choose from to format a table in your document.

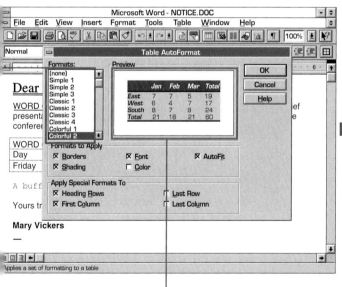

◆ The **Table AutoFormat** ialog box appears.

◆ The **Formats:** box isplays a list of the vailable table designs.

4 Press ↓ or ↑ on your keyboard until the **Preview** box displays the design you want to use (example: **Colorful 2**).

Note: To continue, refer to the next page.

235

FORMAT A TABLE

FORMAT A TABLE (Continued)

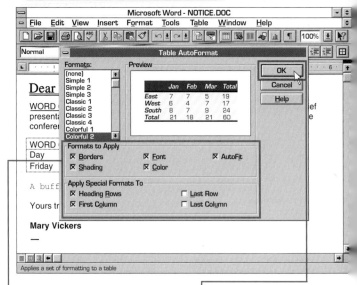

Applies a set of formatting to a table

5 To apply or remove a format, move the mouse ⌖ over an option (example: **Color**) and then press the left button.

Note: ⊠ indicates an option is on.
☐ indicates an option is off.

6 When the **Preview** box displays the desired table appearance, move the mouse ⌖ over **OK** and then press the left button.

236

The Table AutoFormat feature will enhance the appearance of your table.

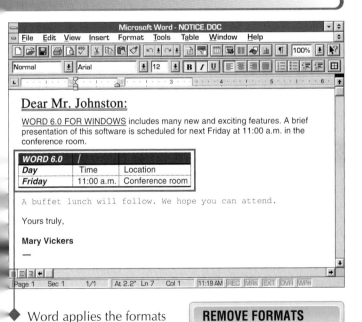

◆ Word applies the formats you selected to the table.

REMOVE FORMATS

To remove the formats from the table, perform steps **1** to **3**, select **(none)** in step **4** and then perform step **6**.

237

MERGE CELLS

MERGE CELLS

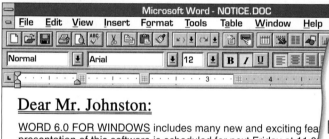

1 Move the mouse I over the first cell you want to join with other cells.

Note: You can only join cells in the same row. You cannot join cells in the same column.

2 Press and hold down the left button as you move the mouse I to highlight the cells you want to join. Then release the button.

You can combine two or more cells in your table to create one large cell.

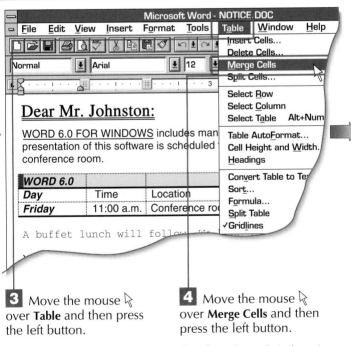

3 Move the mouse ⌖ over **Table** and then press the left button.

4 Move the mouse ⌖ over **Merge Cells** and then press the left button.

Note: To continue, refer to the next page.

239

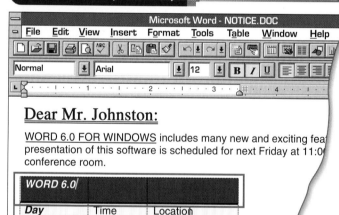

◆ The cells merge into one.

Note: To deselect the cell, move the mouse I outside the table and then press the left button.

◆ If a blank line appears in the row, you can remove the extra line. To do so, position the insertion point to the right of the text in the cell and then press Delete.

The Merge Cells feature is useful when you want to display a title at the top of your table.

SPLIT CELLS

You can split one cell into two or more cells.

1 Position the insertion point in the cell you want to split.

2 Move the mouse 🕂 over **Table** and then press the left button.

3 Move the mouse 🕂 over **Split Cells** and then press the left button. The **Split Cells** dialog box appears.

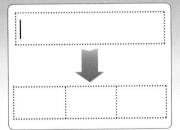

4 Type the number of columns you want to create (example: **3**).

5 Move the mouse 🕂 over **OK** and then press the left button.

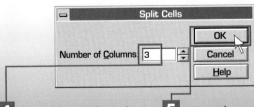

INDEX

INDEX

SIMPLIFIED	SIMPLIFIED EXPANDED	VISUAL POCKETGUIDE
WINDOWS 3.1 SIMPLIFIED *By: maranGraphics* ISBN: 1-56884-652-5 $14.99 USA £13.99 UK	**WINDOWS 3.1 SIMPLIFIED EXPANDED** *By: maranGraphics* ISBN: 1-56884-654-1 $19.99 USA £18.99 UK	**WINDOWS 3.1 VISUAL POCKETGUIDE** *By: maranGraphics* ISBN: 1-56884-650-9 $14.99 USA £13.99 UK
COMPUTERS SIMPLIFIED *By: maranGraphics* ISBN: 1-56884-651-7 $14.99 USA £13.99 UK	**EXCEL 5 SIMPLIFIED EXPANDED** *By: maranGraphics* ISBN: 1-56884-664-9 $19.99 USA £18.99 UK	**EXCEL 5 VISUAL POCKETGUIDE** *By: maranGraphics* ISBN: 1-56884-667-3 $14.99 USA £13.99 UK
WORD 6 FOR WINDOWS SIMPLIFIED *By: maranGraphics* ISBN: 1-56884-659-2 $14.99 USA £13.99 UK	**WORD 6 FOR WINDOWS SIMPLIFIED EXPANDED** *By: maranGraphics* ISBN: 1-56884-660-6 $19.99 USA £18.99 UK	**WORD 6 FOR WINDOWS VISUAL POCKETGUIDE** *By: maranGraphics* ISBN: 1-56884-666-5 $14.99 USA £13.99 UK
MS-DOS 6.2 SIMPLIFIED *By: maranGraphics* ISBN: 1-56884-653-3 $14.99 USA £13.99 UK		

This is what reviewers are saying about maranGraphics' books...

"If you're someone new to computers and 'all thumbs' or just scared of the machines, this series of books will gently guide you through. Nothing could be clearer. They are made for novices."
Peter McWilliams,
Nationally Syndicated Columnist

"This full-color illustrated guide to Windows is a must-have, whether you're a new Windows user or just one looking for easy-to-learn Windows shortcuts."
Inside Microsoft Windows,
The Cobb Group

"...maranGraphics is the greatest thing that has happened to computers since the invention of the PC."
Jim Van Speybroeck,
Data Processing Digest

Order Form
Order Center: (800) 762-2974
(8 a.m.-5 p.m., EST, weekdays) or (317) 895-5260

For Fastest Service: Photocopy This Order
Form and FAX it to: (317) 895-5299

Qty.	ISBN	Title	Price	Total

Shipping & Handling Charges

Subtotal	U.S.	International	International Air Mail
Up to $20.00	Add $3.00	Add $4.00	Add $10.00
$20.01-40.00	$4.00	$5.00	$20.00
$40.01-60.00	$5.00	$6.00	$25.00
$60.01-80.00	$6.00	$8.00	$35.00
Over $80.00	$7.00	$10.00	$50.00

In U.S., shipping is UPS ground or equivalent.
For Rush shipping call (800) 762-2974.

Subtotal _____

CA residents add
applicable sales tax _____

IN and MA residents
add 5% sales tax _____

IL residents add
6.25% sales tax _____

RI residents add
7% sales tax _____

Shipping _____

Total _____

Ship to:

Name _____ Daytime Phone _____

Address _____

City/State/Zip _____

Payment: ❏ Check to IDG Books (US Funds Only)   ❏ Visa

❏ Mastercard   ❏ American Express

Card# _____ Exp._____ Signature_____

Please send this order form to: IDG Books, 3250 North Post Road, Suite 140, Indianapolis, IN 462.
Allow up to 3 weeks for delivery. Thank you!

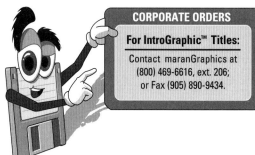

CORPORATE ORDERS

For IntroGraphic™ Titles:

Contact maranGraphics at
(800) 469-6616, ext. 206;
or Fax (905) 890-9434.

IDG BOOKS WORLDWIDE REGISTRATION CARD

Title of this book: WORD 6.0 VISUAL POCKET GUIDE

My overall rating of this book:
❏ Very good [1] ❏ Good [2] ❏ Satisfactory [3] ❏ Fair [4] ❏ Poor [5]

IDG BOOKS

THE WORLD OF COMPUTER KNOWLEDGE

How I first heard about this book:
❏ Found in bookstore; name: [6]
❏ Book review: [7]
❏ Advertisement: [8]
❏ Catalog: [9]
❏ Word of mouth; heard about book from friend, co-worker, etc.: [10]
❏ Other: [11]

What I liked most about this book:

What I would change, add, delete, etc., in future editions of this book:

Other comments:

Number of computer books I purchase in a year: ❏ 1 [12] ❏ 2-5 [13] ❏ 6-10 [14] ❏ More than 10 [15]

I would characterize my computer skills as:
❏ Beginner [16] ❏ Intermediate [17] ❏ Advanced [18] ❏ Professional [19]

I use ❏ DOS [20] ❏ Windows [21] ❏ OS/2 [22] ❏ Unix [23] ❏ Macintosh [24] ❏ Other: [25]_____
(please specify)

I would be interested in new books on the following subjects:
(please check all that apply, and use the spaces provided to identify specific software)

❏ Word processing: [26]   ❏ Spreadsheets: [27]
❏ Data bases: [28]   ❏ Desktop publishing: [29]
❏ File Utilities: [30]   ❏ Money management: [31]
❏ Networking: [32]   ❏ Programming languages: [33]
❏ Other: [34]

I use a PC at (please check all that apply): ❏ home [35] ❏ work [36] ❏ school [37] ❏ other: [38] _____
The disks I prefer to use are ❏ 5.25 [39] ❏ 3.5 [40] ❏ other: [41]_____

I have a CD ROM: ❏ yes [42]   ❏ no [43]

I plan to buy or upgrade computer hardware this year: ❏ yes [44] ❏ no [45]

I plan to buy or upgrade computer software this year: ❏ yes [46] ❏ no [47]

Name: _____ Business title: [48] _____
Type of Business: [49] _____
Address (❏ home [50] ❏ work [51]/Company name: _____)
Street/Suite# _____
City [52]/State [53]/Zipcode [54]: _____ Country [55] _____

❏ **I liked this book!**
You may quote me by name in future IDG Books Worldwide promotional materials.

My daytime phone number is _____

❏ YES!

Please keep me informed about IDG's World
of Computer Knowledge. Send me the latest
IDG Books catalog.

NO POSTAGE
NECESSARY
IF MAILED
IN THE
UNITED STATES

BUSINESS REPLY MAIL
FIRST CLASS MAIL   PERMIT NO. 2605   FOSTER CITY, CALIFORNIA

IDG Books Worldwide
919 E Hillsdale Blvd, STE 400
Foster City, CA 94404-9691